Break of Day

FRENCH MODERNIST LIBRARY

Series Editors:

Mary Ann Caws

Richard Howard

Patricia Terry

ANDRÉ BRETON

Break of Day

(Point du jour)

TRANSLATED BY

Mark Polizzotti & Mary Ann Caws

University of Nebraska Press

Lincoln · London

*Publication of this translation was assisted by a grant
from the French Ministry of Culture.*

Originally published as *Point du jour* by Editions Gallimard, Paris, in 1934.
Copyright © 1934, 1970 by Editions Gallimard.
Translation copyright © 1999 by Mark Polizzotti and Mary Ann Caws.
Foreword copyright © 1999 by Mary Ann Caws.
Preface copyright © 1999 by Mark Polizzotti.

LIBRARY OF CONGRESS CATALOGING-IN-PUBLICATION DATA

Breton, André, 1896–1966.

[Point du jour. English]

Break of day = Point du jour / André Breton;

translated by Mark Polizzotti & Mary Ann Caws.

p.   cm.—(French modernist library)

Includes bibliographical references.

ISBN 0-8032-1259-3 (cl.: alk. paper)

I. Polizzotti, Mark.   II. Caws, Mary Ann.   III. Title.

IV. Title: Point du jour.   V. Series.

PQ2603.R35P613   1999

844'.912—dc21   99-18321

CIP

ISBN 978-0-8032-2084-3 (pa.: alk. paper)

Contents

Foreword

"...what might still take place?"

— ANDRÉ BRETON, on

Paul Eluard's *Capital of Pain*

A PARTICULAR OPTIMISM ATTACHES to the essays gathered here, under the appropriate sign of daybreak. André Breton's sense of mingling elements in a transitional mental space permits him, and now us, to see past more ordinary divisions to a realm he characterized as Surrealist. As day and night, yes and no, life and death meet, confer, and communicate, so, too, can air or fire be of water, visible in the title of Breton's poetry collection *L'air de l'eau* and in the last line of one of his great poems:

> Flame of water guide me to
> The sea of fire

Here, at earliest break of day, assemble various witnesses to the joining of things, proofs of Breton's constant will to start out afresh, from anywhere, on the road or the open sea, going somewhere else.

We believe, says Breton in his essay on Dalí, in a collective credo that was to hold, in those years: "We believe we are winning the case we have brought against reality..." The junctures Surrealism fought for were never the easy ones, political or esthetic, that would have erased differences in honor of the principle of sitting down in comfortable consumerism, like Rimbaud's dreadful "*assis*" — those figures of a bourgeois comfort befitting the furniture store instead of the storehouse of the imagination. Breton's invocation of the marvelous in its refusal of the easy inspires his pagan prayer for Dalí's continuing nay-saying:

> May it please the powers whose envoy he is in the world and among us that he forever keep his eyes closed to the miserable plans for bridges that greed and spite will conspire to make him cast across the sparkling, unapproachable, and magnetic river...

What the Surrealist artist invokes above all is a power of disturbance, as in Max Ernst's requirement of the Hundred Headless Woman, in whose universe "things are called upon to do something other than what's usually expected."

In the late twenties and the early thirties, did life feel different from now? Have the seventy years, so quickly passed from his moment to ours, changed the way things look and are? Just after the "heroic" period of Surrealism in the early twenties, when manifestoes had to be major and gestures large, this second period is a time of vigor, of judgments passed and taken. Surrealist courage calls for a challenge sufficiently sharp to welcome it. The Surrealist eye, in art as in politics, kept its vision clear and its esthetic sense unclouded. Nothing in these essays conveys the feeling of twilight, that other time when two moments join. There is instead the sense of starting out, with things just beginning to come clear.

MARY ANN CAWS

Preface:
In the Harsh Light of Dawn

ROM THEIR OFTEN IMPRESSIVE breadth and imposing erudition, one would be hard put to recognize that the pieces in this collection were written during one of the most difficult periods Breton ever faced. Unlike his first volume of essays, *The Lost Steps* (1924), which chronicles Surrealism's gestation, *Break of Day* is a record of the movement's, and the author's, early maturity. This is the work of a man with dawn already at his back, ready to face the broad daylight of what he has wrought. Only in certain passages – Breton's embattled defense of the Surrealists' leftist convictions, his bitter assessments of Mayakovsky's tragic despair or Achim von Arnim's tortured marriage – can we glimpse just how harsh the road ahead was proving to be.

Break of Day picks up in the wake of Surrealism's emergence, following the publication of the first *Manifesto of Surrealism* in 1924 and the flurry of public activity that continued throughout the fall of that year. By the time of the last essay, the dispirited "Automatic Message," written almost a decade later – the volume itself was published in July 1934, when Breton was thirty-eight years old – the author had jettisoned many of his early companions, all but given up trying to work with the Communists, and been forced to question many of Surrealism's basic assumptions. He had also suffered a painful divorce and weathered a particularly trying love affair, and he now found himself demoralized and alone, despite the presence of a few friends and his growing reputation in literary circles. Even the telephone, that last-resort lifeline to the outside world, was no longer available: too poor to pay his phone bill, Breton had had his service disconnected.

In many ways, in fact, and despite the greater sweep and mastery of these essays, this is a much more solitary book than *The Lost Steps.* Gone for the most part is the constant sense of shared adventure, the frequent dropping of friends' names (mainly unknown at the time, but always given with the belief that they were soon *to be reckoned with*) that endow the earlier volume with its patina of brash optimism. Here adolescence has made way for the weight and disillusionments of adulthood. And if Breton still finds things to celebrate – Max Ernst's collage-novels, Dalí's hallucinatory paintings, Picasso's "extra-pictorial" objects among them – more often than not the tone of these essays suggests a besieged monarch struggling to preserve his tiny principality from both outside aggression and internal strife. The legalistic flavor of some of his titles ("Burial Denied," "In Self-Defense," "Psychiatry Standing before Surrealism") is no coincidence.*

*   *   *

Breton's horizon was already beginning to cloud as he put the finishing touches to the first article in this volume. A prolongation of the half-lyrical, half-discursive prose that shortly before had marked the first *Manifesto,* his "introduction" to a never-written

---

* As to the book's overall title – *Point du jour* in French – despite its clear suggestion of "dawning" and "a new day," one critic has made a persuasive case for an alternate interpretation, namely that Breton is taking stock *(faire le point)* of Surrealism's day-to-day situation. And indeed, many of these essays function as a means of dotting the i's, of clarifying the movement's positions and answering others' objections and criticisms—though this in no way detracts from the title's more immediate connotation. See Gérard Legrand, *Breton* (Paris: Les Dossiers Belfond, 1977), p. 127.

discourse was completed in early 1925 – by which time Breton's emotional well-being, and his three-year marriage to Simone Kahn, was being sorely tested by the irruption in his life of a "very attractive sorceress, with the voluptuous and seductive eyes of the Queen of Sheba." Lise Meyer, a socialite with literary pretensions (she later published under the name Lise Deharme), had met Breton during her recent visit to the Bureau of Surrealist Research, an office-cum-meeting place meant to attract likeminded individuals to the movement. Wealthy and extremely flirtatious, the small, dark-haired Lise so entranced the normally imposing Breton at that first meeting that he found himself literally unable to speak. Sensing an easy conquest, she found it no great task, and apparently no small pleasure, to tease the renowned Surrealist leader into a hopeless infatuation that would last for the next three years.

But while certain melancholy passages of "Introduction to the Discourse" might be said to reflect his nascent, and ultimately unrequited, passion for Lise, there is little explicit trace of it in these essays. Instead, Breton channeled his emotional frustrations into a more public disgruntlement with the French Communist Party (PCF) and specifically with its refusal to credit Surrealism's attempts at making common cause against the reigning class structure.

That a body of politically oriented, relatively mainstream functionaries should look askance upon overtures from some obscure poets with a marked anarchistic bent, that they should raise eyebrows at the Surrealists' stated desire (as Breton put it) to act as independent guardians against the party's "most characteristic impostures and deviations," and that they should take umbrage at Breton's specific and vehement attacks on certain party doctrines and organisms should come as no surprise to anyone. Yet from his first discovery of Soviet Communism in 1925 to his final disenchantment with it ten years later, Breton doggedly maintained that Communism had as much to gain from Surrealism's philosophical perspectives as the latter did from the Communists' pragmatic savvy, and he met the party's rebuffs of his support with wounded bafflement. For Breton, no economic or political revolution could successfully be staged if one did not first revise man's psychological and spiritual orientations – did not, in other words, pull him away from the deadening confines of the wage-system mentality and of the assembly-line artworks that mirrored and supported it – and he failed to understand how the Communists could so lightly dismiss Surrealism's contribution in that regard. His critiques in "In Self-Defense" aim at a humanly consequential alternative to the party's rigid Stalinism, even as his review of the "proletarian literature contest" sponsored by the Communist newspaper *L'Humanité* proposes a more rewarding literary curriculum for the working class than their standard mind-numbing fare. But the party was less interested in critiques (however well-intentioned) than in loyal supporters, and Breton's arguments, despite their impassioned force, ended up only deepening his rift with the PCF.

At times, Breton's twin sources of frustration, the personal and the ideological, combine in a single essay, and nowhere in *Break of Day* is this more evident than in "*Lyubovnaya lodka razbilas o byt*," his editorial on the circumstances and aftermath of Vladimir Mayakovsky's suicide over an unhappy love affair. Breton had met the great Soviet poet in late 1928, introduced by the writer Elsa Triolet (soon to become the wife of his sidekick Louis Aragon). Although their lack of a common language had kept communications between the two men rudimentary, Breton highly esteemed Mayakovsky as a poet and a human being. His posthumous defense of the Russian, however, reflects not only his personal admiration, but also the more private drama infusing his life at the time.

The previous year, after long maintaining Breton's courtship at arm's length, Lise Meyer had finally ended the game by marrying radio pioneer Paul Deharme. Several weeks later, Breton met and fell violently in love with a young beauty named Suzanne Muzard, who at the time was the mistress of the novelist Emmanuel Berl. "Tall, slender, gracefully shaped, with regular, slightly Nordic features" (according to one Surrealist), Suzanne had grown up, like Breton, in one of the industrial suburbs north of Paris. Although she was now living with Berl, within days her new paramour had persuaded her to run away with him to the south of France. "Suzanne is utterly exquisite," the besotted lover raved to his wife from a Toulon hotel. "She has told me marvelous stories that I was born to hear and that you would love. Truly marvelous stories. Not for a moment has she been anything but what I imagined her to be... maybe a thousand times better. This is the first time in a week I've left her side for even ten minutes."

But the honeymoon was short-lived, for the woman had needs and demands of her own – first and foremost that Breton divorce Simone and marry her, which Breton, despite his enchantment with Suzanne, was unprepared to do. What followed was a three-year cataclysm that kept Breton teetering between rapture and desperation, as he and his lover went from acrimonious break-ups to tearful reconciliations, and Suzanne fled repeatedly from Breton to Berl and back again. The strains of this love affair would have no small impact on Breton's public actions during that period, notably the spate of purges that decimated the Surrealist ranks in the late 1920s and the vituperative salvoes that comprise much of the *Second Manifesto of Surrealism*, the most pugnacious of his major works.

Finally, in late 1928 – at almost exactly the moment he met Mayakovsky – Breton acceded to Suzanne's request and filed for divorce, only to find that Suzanne had just married Berl instead (which did little to change the pattern of their relations over the next two years). Given the coincidence of these events with the Russian's visit, as well as the similarity of Breton's and Mayakovsky's emotional states around the time of the poet's suicide in April 1930 and the severity of the Communists' ensuing attacks on both Surrealism and Mayakovsky, it is little wonder that Breton, in his polemical obituary, seems to be talking as much about himself as about the late Soviet bard.

A polemic of a different nature governs Breton's open letter to André Rolland de Renéville, written in February 1932. Renéville, a poet and critic who had earned Breton's respect (plus an invitation to join Surrealism that he had ultimately declined), represented the second strain of criticism brought against Surrealism since its turn toward Communist politics. For while the leftists denigrated the Surrealists as bourgeois intellectuals playing at revolution, the movement's literary proponents, such as Renéville, deplored its abandonment of automatic writing and "the conquest of the mind" for the more mundane concerns of political activism. In response, Breton defended his attempts to reconcile poetry with social action, Surrealism's embrace of dialectical materialism, and its stated will to "act upon the facts" of the outside world. What is curious about Breton's position is not so much its association of pure poetry with radical politics but the fact that, in the same month, he was defending his friend Aragon and the latter's propaganda poem "Red Front" (for which

Aragon had been indicted for sedition), on the grounds that "Red Front" was, after all, just a poem, and therefore not subject to prosecution. The argument was disingenuous at best, and the fact is that Breton's rebuttal to Renéville is a much more authentic expression of his thinking on the subject. As it happened, Breton's attempted defense of "Red Front" backfired on all counts: not only did it do nothing to help Aragon's legal entanglement but it further alienated Breton from the Communists and, worst of all, cost him his friendship with the man who had been his staunchest ally for nearly fifteen years.

Indeed, by the time the last essays in this book were written, Breton had lost virtually all of his former associates – those whose names were so proudly trumpeted in *The Lost Steps* and many others in their wake. Of the movement's early members, only a handful remained: Max Ernst, Yves Tanguy, Benjamin Péret, and especially Paul Eluard, who for the next several years would be Breton's closest friend. Otherwise, as Eluard's wife wrote in a letter, he was "*all alone,*" and "truly unhappy."

Given this, it is understandable that the tenor of his essays from 1933, particularly his presentation of Achim von Arnim and his reevaluation of "the automatic message," is one of sorrow and discontent. The lengthy piece on Arnim, written to introduce the republication of the German writer's *Strange Tales,* shuttles uneasily between Breton's laudatory portrait of Arnim as a preeminent (if undervalued) German Romantic and his harrowing picture of the man's home life. As with the essay on Mayakovsky, it takes little effort of imagination to see behind Breton's caustic portrayal of Bettina von Arnim, whose long-standing infatuation with Goethe (Emmanuel Berl?) was pursued at her husband's expense, a bitter memory of his years with Suzanne. The fact that this edition of *Strange Tales* was being illustrated by the painter

Valentine Hugo, with whom Breton had only recently ended an unsatisfying "rebound" relationship, no doubt added to his evident feelings of solidarity with Arnim.

Breton's personal stake in "The Automatic Message" is higher still, for what he is calling into question here is the cornerstone of Surrealism itself. In the movement's early years, the terms "automatic writing" and "Surrealist writing" had been used interchangeably, to designate the spontaneous verbal outflow that Breton hoped would both lead to a true "state of grace" and, in terms of artistic pretensions, "cleanse the literary stables definitively." But as he was forced to note, the "history of automatic writing in Surrealism" over the previous decade was "one of continual misfortune," inspiring internecine rivalries and writerly vanity that had finally undermined his loftier ambitions for automatism and its liberating potential.

Throughout the summer and fall of 1933, Breton spent his days in painstaking research for "The Automatic Message" at the fusty Bibliothèque Nationale, his evenings with a dwindling band of Surrealist faithfuls, his nights awake in the sweltering heat of his lonely studio on Rue Fontaine. In a moment of comic ingenuity, he and Eluard resolved to pay each other a one-franc fine for every complaint uttered, in hopes of stemming their tendency toward discouraging words. But reasons for discouragement were many at the time, and the wry note on which Breton ends his essay, and the book, belie his attempts throughout to salvage the first decade of Surrealism's existence.

And yet, Breton's particular gift was never entirely to lose sight, despite the storms he and his movement endured in those ten years, of the dawn light always just breaking over his shoulder. It is this seemingly endless capacity to derive wonderment from a Picasso sculpture or Eluard poem; to maintain faith in Communism's basic tenets (despite their misuse by the French and Soviet parties) or in automatism as *"the* vehicle of revelation" (despite its mishandling by certain poets); to look constantly, and against all odds, toward the promise of a new morning that endows Breton's prose with its inspiring vigor. Dark as his perspectives might sometimes be, he clearly recognized, in placing this collection under the sign of renewed hope, that the miracle of resurrection lies squarely here below, and that every day it is ours for the taking.

MARK POLIZZOTTI

A Note on the Translation

Each of these essays was first rendered by one of the translators then submitted to the other for revisions and comments. Although the end result is, therefore, a true collaboration, each piece unavoidably bears to some extent the stamp of its original translator. To clarify matters, we would like to specify that "Paul Eluard's *Capital of Pain*," "The X..., Y... Exhibit," "Notice to the Reader of *The Hundred Headless Woman*," "The First Dalí Exhibit," "Picasso in His Element," and "The Faces of Women" were primarily translated by Mary Ann Caws, and the others primarily by Mark Polizzotti.

Break of Day

Introduction
to the Discourse on
the Paucity of Reality

W IRELESS": THERE'S A WORD that has all too recently entered our vocabulary, a locution whose rise has been too rapid for it not to contain many of the dreams of our epoch, for it not to reveal to me one of the very few specifically new determinations of our minds. Feeble reference points such as these are what sometimes give me the illusion of attempting a great adventure, of looking to some small degree like a gold prospector: I seek the gold of time. So what do they evoke, these words I chose? Barely the coastal sands, a few field spiders intertwined in the hollow of a willow tree – a willow or the sky, for no doubt it's a wide-range antenna, then islands, nothing but islands... Crete, where I must be Theseus, but Theseus forever caught in his crystal labyrinth.

Wireless telegraph, wireless telephone, wireless imagination, as they say. The induction is easy, but I also believe it's legitimate. Invention, human discovery, the faculty we are so parsimoniously granted, over time, to know and possess things no one had any inkling of before us, is bound to throw us into great confusion. On the side of truth, this modesty would alarm us less if it did not occasionally pretend to yield up, abandon to us the tiniest of its secrets, only to revert quickly to its hesitations. The ill humor of most men who ultimately stopped falling for these paltry revelations, who contented themselves once and for all with only invariable data, the way one looks at mountains or the sea – classical minds, in short – is what nonetheless keeps them from taking full advantage of a life that, granted, does not essentially differ from all past lives but that on the other hand must not be so vain as to set itself such limits: André Breton (1896–19..).

I am in the hall of a castle, my dark lantern in hand, and one by one I illuminate the sparkling suits of armor. Don't go thinking it's some evildoer's trick. One of these suits of armor seems almost my size; if only I could put it on and find in it a little of the consciousness of a fourteenth-century man. O eternal theater, you demand that not only to play another's role, but even to dictate that role, we should take on his disguise; that the mirror before which we pose should reflect back a foreign image of ourselves. Imagination can do anything, except make us look, despite our natural appearance, like someone other than ourselves. Literary speculation is illicit as soon as it sets before an author characters that he deems right or wrong, after having created them from whole cloth. "Speak for yourself," I would tell him. "Speak about yourself; you'll tell me so much more. I do not recognize your power of life or death over these pseudo-human beings who spring armed and disarmed from your fancy. Just leave me your memoirs and have done with it. Give me real names; prove to me that you've never held sway over your protagonists." I don't like it when people shilly-shally, nor when they hide. I am in the hall of a castle, my dark lantern in hand, and one by one I illuminate the sparkling suits of armor. Later, in this same hall – who knows? – someone will casually put on my suit. From pedestal to pedestal, the great silent colloquy will continue:

THE ARMOR'S COLLOQUY

"I understand, do you hear? How can one still suffer the galloping of horses in the countryside? Even for them, the sun of the dead might well shine; the living always rush hell for leather to help what is beyond help. They make it an affair of State."

"They ended up convincing themselves that the life they were living was neither their first nor their last. Doing something once, they said, doesn't prove anything. As for us, let's knock on green wood."

A WOMAN'S VOICE: "Here are a few who are lingering in couples. Pity on them alone! Suits of armor, more sparkle to you; lovers, more pleasure to you."

"Can one being be present for another being?"

ANOTHER WOMAN'S VOICE: "I existed only for twenty hawthorn bushes. It's from them, alas, that this charming corselet is made. But I've also known pure light: the love of love."

I: "The fearless soul plunges into a land with no escape, where one's eyes open without weeping. One wanders there to no purpose; one obeys without anger. One can see behind oneself without turning around. Finally I ponder beauty without veils, the earth without stains, the medal without a reverse. No longer do I beg forgiveness for nothing, without belief. No one can shut the door with no hinges. What good is it setting these harmless traps in the woods of the heart? No doubt a day without bread would not be so long."

. . . .

None of this settles anything. Just let me lift my head from my hands and the din of futile things begins to deafen me once again. I am in the world, quite in the world, and even darkened right now by daylight's end. I know that in Paris, on the boulevards, the beautiful lighted signs are beginning to appear. These signs occupy a large place in my daily walks, and yet the truth is that they convey only things that annoy me. At my window, I am thinking, too, of the roughly equal distribution of human beings in private or public places, from one day to the next. How can one explain, for instance, why a normally full auditorium should never be nearly empty even for one evening, simply because everyone had other things to do? (I'm talking about theaters where the seats are very cheap or free.) Why do trains, in a given time of year, always carry more or less the same number of passengers? What is striking in such cases is the absence of coincidence. I indulge in remarks like this all the time, which might seem ludicrous but which give an accurate picture of the obstacles that anyone's thought might have to overcome. There is also the importance I'm forced to attach to heat and cold – in short, the entire process of continual distraction that makes me abandon one idea per friend, one friend per idea; that forces me to move around when I'm writing, to interrupt myself in the middle of a sentence, as if I needed reassurance that a given object was in its correct place in the room, that one or another of my articulations was working right. The existence (duly noted in advance) of this bouquet I'm about to smell or this catalog I'm leafing through should be enough for me: but no. I have to assure myself of its reality, as they say, to make contact with it. The mistake would be to see this mimic as merely expressive. Despite its multiple accidents, my thought makes its own way and doesn't seem to suffer overly from betrayal, if betrayal it is. "Take it easy," she tells me. "I won't keep you here." And so I allow myself to read the newspapers (and, I admit, very few books), to talk to strangers, to play, sometimes even to laugh, to caress a woman, to be bored, to enter a public square: in short, to take outside of this thought my few pleasures where I find them. As she is harder to subjugate than I; she likes it when I tell her of the strange, daily fascination that these places, actions, things, *this lowest common denominator of men* exert on me. What independence she enjoys! She is strong, too, like everything that will remain of me. She is darker than night, and in vain do I try to occupy her with things that seem to occur very far away, in her absence; with what I tell her is a succession of wonders, so that I'll be sure she's listening to me, like the sad and beautiful queen she is:

THE SUCCESSION OF WONDERS

"Wonders, Madam – but first let me describe this shipwreck for you. Our vessel was carrying everything you can imagine as most ours, most precious. There was a plaster Virgin whose halo, to perfect the resemblance, was made of gossamer, so that it shone with the dew. There was a completely white artificial fly that I had stolen from a dead fisherman in a dream, yes, in a dream, and that I spent hours watching float on the water I'd poured into a blue bowl: it was the bait I was saving for the unknown. There was what might come from the bowels of the earth, what might fall from the sky. Healing bushes, the scent of great hyacinths indifferent to the climate reached all the way to the bridge. We had opened the heavy crates so as to see everything. We had also distributed moral guises. The collar of grace was composed only of two pearls called breasts. There was genius, which wasn't only a guise but also a dazzling promise. A couple of birds, by far the rarest, which changed shape with the winds, left the musical instruments far behind – even in this regard.

"By what latitude did it seem to us that the land we were rushing toward retreated the more we approached it, and that instead of reaching it, we had broken the sea of glass? This, Madam, is what I could not tell you. The birds with their cursed song! At that point they flew away sadly, giving no solace. The antagonism of genius and grace, though it lasted but an instant, had been enough to make the flowers virtual. The bridge was made of fallow earth and all that remained, on both sides of the vessel, in the transparency of the waves, was the inverted image of the great hyacinths indifferent to the climate. The Virgin had lost her halo in the storm and the solitary white fly, extraordinarily phosphorescent, rocked in its night-blue bowl.

"You will thank me, Madam, for sparing you the relation of our cries of despair when we felt that we would miss everything, that at every step what might exist destroys what does exist, that absolute solitude gradually vaporizes what we touch. It is you, isn't it, who enter the colorless aviary; it's you who consigns the tides to this damning efflorescence.

"The wonder, Madam, is that on the shore where you cast us up half-dead, we retain the awestruck memory of our disaster. There are no more living birds, no more real flowers. Every creature harbors the disappointment of knowing itself to be unique. Even what is born of it does not belong to it and, moreover, is anything born of it? Does it know? The wonder, again, is that the engulfing of all that splendor should be a matter of time, let's say almost of age, and that one day we might discover a wreck on the sand where we know there was nothing the day before.

"I bring you the most beautiful and perhaps only remnant of my shipwreck. In this chest that I deliver to you and for which I don't have the key sleeps the disarming idea of presence and absence in love."

. . . .

Here the magnetic needle goes crazy. Everything that obstinately indicates the deserted north no longer knows which way to turn before the dawn. On the whole, the enigma of the sexes reconciles the wise and the insane. The sky falling on the heads of the Gauls, the grass ruined by the hooves of the Huns' steeds – nothing from the slippery Thermopylae to the marvelous formula "After me, the Flood" can better lead us to the edge of our precipice. Museums at night, spacious and lit up like music halls, preserve the chaste and audacious nude from the great whirlwind.

I, a man, now watch that woman sleeping. We await the end of the world, of the external world, from one moment to the next. We are the ones who have braved the consequences from the start, putting forth the fatal character of our minds. What should I care what they say about me, since I am not the one speaking, to whom I am speaking, and in whose interest we are speaking? I forget, I speak about what I've already forgotten. I've systematically forgotten everything that ever happened to me, good or bad, if not indifferent. Only the indifferent is admirable. The terrible psychological law of compensations, which I have never seen formulated – and by virtue of which apparently we will soon pay dearly for a moment of lucidity, pleasure, or happiness; not to mention that our worst collapse, our greatest despair will gain us immediate revenge, and that the regular alternation of these two states, as in manic-depressive psychosis, presupposes a rigorously equal intensity of our good and evil emotions – the terrible psychological law of compensations leaves indifference (in the balance of the world, the only thing not subject to flaws) by the wayside. It is toward indifference that I have tried to exercise my memory, toward fables without moral, neutral impressions, incomplete statistics... And yet I, a man, now watch that woman sleeping. A woman's sleep is an apotheosis. Do you see this red sheet bordered by a wide band of black lace? Strange bed!

Is it my fault if women sleep beneath the stars, even as they claim to keep us near them in their luxurious bedchambers? They hold over us an incredible power of failure, and I am flattered to include myself in this. To include myself like a lake with mayflies. The lake must be charmed by the incomparable brevity of their lives, and I envy the changing perspectives of the woman for whom the future is never the beyond; the woman who knits her brow at my calculations, and who is sure that I will except her from the pillage, sure that she will be spared the extermination I'm contemplating. She is not angry (on the contrary) at the feeble resistance to my desire for the unreal both by other men and by everything our love could easily do without.

To love each other, even if only a few days remained; to love each other because we are the only ones left after that famous earthquake, and no one can ever free us because we are buried under too much rubble. Only this recourse remains: to love each other. I have never imagined a more beautiful end to my life. Just think, we would no longer have to make allowances. A few square yards would suffice – oh! I know you won't agree with me, but if only you loved me! And besides, it's kind of what is happening to us. Paris collapsed yesterday; we are very low, very low, where there is hardly any room. We have no food or water – you who were afraid of prison! Before long it will be over: yes, we wish we had a weapon to use on the third or fourth day, but there you have it! And yet, think about it, what can't be accomplished by a union such as ours? You are mine for perhaps the first time. You will never leave again; no longer will you have the choice of making me miss you for a few hours, or even for a second. Don't bother, we're shut in on all sides, take my word for it.

And to love each other as long as we can, because I, who accepted the augur of this formidable collapse, stopped wishing for it quite so much the first time I saw you. Our next-to-last candle is fading; we won't light the other until our lives are almost at an end. It will be better, believe me. Come closer, closer still. Is it you? How we desired this obliviousness to everything else! Do you remember? You no longer wanted to dance. You wanted me to fill the time you were kept from me by writing to you, isn't that so? Now we are delivered to ourselves for all eternity. Night is falling. What, are you crying? I'm afraid you don't really love me.

. . . .

Ghost stories, tales of horror, terrifying dreams, prophecies, I leave you all. Rigid mathematicians, attracted by this blackboard (as I might have expected), have taken advantage of the woman's disappearance to pose the problem of my illusion:

A PROBLEM

"Given that the author of these pages, who is not quite twenty-nine years old, has, from the 7th to the 10th of January 1925 (the present date), contradicted himself a hundred times on a crucial point, namely, the value that should be granted to reality – a value somewhere between 0 and ∞ – we can wonder how much more definite he will be eleven years and forty days from now. In case that reality is positive, say also for roughly how many persons he has written this, knowing that poets have one-third as many readers as philosophers, and philosophers two hundred times fewer readers than novelists."

Fine – I can see they respect my doubt, that they treat my sensitivity with care. Still, what a horrible problem! Each day I live, each action I commit, each representation that occurs to me as if from nowhere, makes me feel like a fraud. By writing, I pass, like a smuggler at nightfall, all the instruments needed for the war I wage against myself. Just see how I want to place all my bets on the other side, and how my defeat is my own doing. Let's face it: whatever they might have written on the subject, two leaves from the same tree are rigorously alike; they're even the same leaf. I have only one word to say. If two drops of water can resemble each other so closely, it means there's only one drop of water. A thread that repeats and crosses over itself makes silk. The staircase I walk up never has more than one step. There is only one color: white. The vanished Great Wheel has only one spoke. From there to the first and only ray of sunlight* is but a single step.

Where does that will to reduction lead, that terror of what someone before me called the demon Plural? Many times people looking at photographs of me have taken it into their heads to tell me, "It's you," or, "It isn't you." (Then who could it be? Who could succeed me in the free exercise of my personality?) There are others who study my face, claiming to recognize me, to have seen me somewhere, especially in places I've never been – which is much worse. I remember one sinister joker who, one evening near Châtelet, stopped the passers-by along the quay – if they weren't alone he roughly took one of them aside – and asked point-blank: "What is your name?" I suppose that almost every-

* Untranslatable pun on the word *rayon*, which means both "spoke" and "ray." [*trans.*]

one told him their names. He thanked them tersely and walked away. In the small group that my friends and I formed, I wasn't the one he chose. I admire the courage of that man, who could offer himself such a show for free, the way I admire the courage of a few other famous practical jokers, able to act without witnesses at the expense of one or several individuals. All the same, how alone one must feel! I'm also thinking of poetry, which is a practical joke of another kind, perhaps the most serious kind.

These days it displays such particular demands. See the importance it attaches to the possible, and its love of the implausible. What is, what might be – how insufficient it finds all that! Nature, it denies your reign; things, what could it care about your properties? It knows no rest so long as it has not run its negativistic hand over the entire universe. It's the eternal dare of Gérard de Nerval walking a lobster on a leash near the Palais-Royal. Poetic abuses are not nearly over. The Doe with bronze hooves and golden horns, which I carry wounded on my shoulders to Paris or Mycenæ, transfigures the world as I pass. The changes occur so quickly that I hardly have time to notice. In 1918, on the ward in the Val-de-Grâce that they euphemistically called the *"Quatrième Fiévreux"* and that at the time was an entire poem in itself – in that ward where I had been assigned to keep watch – on some evenings I saw a middle-aged gentleman of modest appearance inside his padded cell, whose knife and laces they had taken the precaution of removing, whom they often forgot to feed, and who they frequently made sure had nothing on him but some ratty trousers, his hospital blouse, and the horrible blue coat with one red sleeve that constituted the uniform of the insane. Well, you won't believe me, but when we were alone that man, who had come to trust me, unfurled to my ever renewed surprise huge flags, including a German and a Russian flag, which he pulled from who knows where. One night he even sent two doves flying out before my eyes, and for our next meeting he promised me rabbits. I stopped seeing him around that time, and to this day I regret not having tried harder to find out who he was. I insist that this anecdote is strictly true, and I hope it doesn't make me appear too suggestible. I can't escape the thought that this bizarre magician, who hardly ever spoke, was suffering from something other than an incomprehensible lapse in surveillance.

Our own surveillance, as I've since noted, is no better. Poetically speaking, our senses, with the just barely acceptable nature of their data, are a reference that can't satisfy us. Render therefore unto Porphyry the things that are Porphyry's: "Do varieties and species exist in themselves or only in the mind? And in the first case, are they corporeal or incorporeal? In a word, do they exist apart from tangible things or are they to be confused with them?" The record has been set straight once and for all: "I clearly see the horse; but I do not see horseness."

What remains are words, since the same dispute is still ongoing. Words are likely to group together by particular affinities, and as a result they constantly recreate the world on its old model. Everything happens as if a concrete reality existed outside of the individual – what am I saying, as if this reality were immutable. On the level of pure and simple observation, if this is how we envision it, we need an absolute certainty to advance something new, something liable to clash with common sense. The famous *E pur, si muove!*, which Galileo muttered under his breath after recanting his doctrine, remains forever apropos. Does every man of today, eager to conform to the directions of his time, feel he could describe the latest biological discoveries, for example, or the theory of relativity?

But I've already said that words, by the nature we grant them, deserve to play a far more decisive role. Nothing is gained by modifying them since, just as they are, they respond so promptly to our call. It's already enough for criticism to concern itself with the laws presiding over their assembly. Doesn't the mediocrity of our universe stem essentially from our powers of enunciation? Poetry, in its driest seasons, has often given us ample proof: what a riot of starry skies, precious stones, and dead leaves. Thank God, a slow but certain reaction against all this has started building in people's minds. Things said and repeated are now running up against a solid barrier. *They* are what bound us to that common universe. It is through them that we acquired our taste for money, our restrictive fears, our love of the "fatherland," our horror of our own destiny. I believe it isn't too late to reconsider that disappointment, inherent in the words that we have used so poorly up to now. What should prevent me from mixing up the order of words, and so from violating the merely apparent existence of things! Language can and must be severed from its bondage. No more descriptions from nature, no more studies of mores. Silence, so that I may pass where no one has ever passed, silence! – After you, my beautiful language.

In linguistic matters, the aim (we are told) is to make oneself understood. Understood! Understood by myself, no doubt, when I listen to myself like a small child demanding the rest of a fairy tale. Take warning: I know the meaning of all my words and I *naturally* observe the rules of syntax (which is not, as certain morons believe, a discipline). Given this, I can't see why it should raise any eyebrows if I say that the most satisfying image of the earth I can create for myself at this moment is a paper hoop. If such nonsense has never been proclaimed before, first of all it's because it isn't nonsense. Furthermore, no one can ask me to justify any such statement, or else I demand the context. It once happened that someone, in a critical commentary, was dishonest enough to draw up a table of some of the images offered by one of our greatest living poets. In it, we read:

Morrow of the caterpillar in ball dress means: butterfly.

Breast of crystal means: flagon, etc.

No, sir, *it means nothing of the kind.* Stick your butterfly back in your flagon. You may be sure that what Saint-Pol-Roux said is exactly what he meant.

Let's not forget that only our belief in a certain practical necessity keeps us from according poetic speech a value equal to the one we accord, for example, the speech of an explorer. Human fetishism, which needs to try on the white helmet, to caress the fur bonnet, listens to the tale of our expeditions with an entirely different ear. It must absolutely believe that *this has happened.* It was to respond to this desire for perpetual verification that I recently suggested manufacturing, if possible, some of the objects that one approaches only in dreams – objects that seem wholly unjustified from the viewpoint of both usefulness and enjoyment. A few nights ago, in my sleep, at an outdoor market near Saint-Malo, I put my hands on a rather curious book. The spine of this book was comprised of a wooden gnome whose white beard, styled in Assyrian fashion, descended to his feet. The statue was of normal thickness, though this wouldn't have prevented anyone from turning the pages of the book, which were made of thick black wool. I hastened to acquire it and, upon awakening, I regretted not finding it by my bedside. It would be relatively easy to reconstruct. I'd like to put a few such objects into circulation; their fate seems to me eminently problematic and disturbing. I would attach a copy to each of my books, as a gift to certain select persons.

Who knows whether, in this way, I might help ruin those concrete and hateful trophies; whether I might greatly discredit those "reasonable" creatures and things? There would be highly complicated machines that would remain of no use. We would draw up meticulously detailed plans for enormous cities that, numerous as we are, we would feel forever powerless to build, but that would at least put all present and future capitals in their place. Absurd and highly perfected automata, which would never do anything like anyone else, would be assigned to give us a correct idea of action.

Will poetic creations soon be expected to assume this tangible character, to displace the boundaries of so-called reality in such a singular fashion? It would be better for us to stop ignoring the hallucinatory power of certain images, or the veritable gift for evocation that certain individuals possess (independent of their recall). The God that inhabits us is nowhere near taking his seventh-day rest; we have not gotten beyond the very first pages of Genesis. It is entirely up to us, perhaps, to build the foundations of our new earthly paradise on the ruins of the old world. Nothing has yet been lost, for we recognize from various signs that the great illumination is forging its path. The peril in which reason (in the most general and debatable sense of the word) puts us, by subjecting works of the mind to its unalterable dogmas, by depriving us of the right to choose the least damaging means of expression: this peril has in no way been eliminated. Those miserable proctors, who stick with us even after we've left school, are still intruding into our homes, our lives. They make sure that we always call a spade *a spade* and, since after all we put a good face on it, they don't necessarily hand us over to the galley of asylums and jails. Still, let's hope that someone rids us of those functionaries as quickly as possible... Equally horrible to me is the idea of a bed of stones or a bed of feathers: what can I say, I can only sleep on a bed of elder marrow. Try one out yourself. Comfortable, isn't it? But if we get off on this foot, where will it lead us? Can't you feel that this bed – oh, a simple thing! except they don't make them – suddenly appears full of enticements? that already you have stopped preferring yours? So you don't have so many prejudices after all about the correct raw materials for making a bed. *In reality,* do I sleep on a bed made of elder marrow? Enough! I don't know: it must be true in some way, since I say so.

Autosuggestion or suggestion – don't make me laugh. Which is more a simple game of my mind, an inconsistent reflection: the passage of "Valentine, the Rubber King" in his automotive carriage or those white bottles placed behind the door that make the night-blooming mirabilis close? I claim that one *is* just as much as the other, no more no less.

According to me, nothing is inadmissible. The frog who tried to become bigger than the ox burst apart only in the fabulist's short memory. As a child, I enjoyed believing that the roles had been reversed; that the ox, initially, must have been the smaller animal, the size of a ladybug, who one day tried to become, and became, larger than the frog. It seemed impossible to me that a will, even one so animal and so childish, should not be carried out to perfection.

THE STRANGE DIVERSION

Latin civilization has had its day, and for my part, I ask that we unanimously forego trying to save it. It now seems no more than the last rampart of bad faith, old age, and cowardice. Compromise, ruse, promises of calm, vacant mirrors, selfishness, military dictatorships, the reappearance of the Unbelievers, the defense of congregations, the eight-hour workday, more burials than in the plague years, sports – there's nothing left but to give it all up. If I show any concern for my own determination, it's not so I can fatalistically endure the vulgar consequences of the whim that caused me to be born in such-and-such a place. Let others be attached to their families, their countries, even to the earth; that kind of emulation is foreign to me. The aspects of my being that I have most loved are the ones that offered the greatest contrast with its litigious exterior, and I have never worried about my inner equilibrium. I would even say that this is why I still let myself take an interest in public life and, by writing, sacrifice a bit of my own life to it. To put it plainly, then, I said it out loud (and for the moment, kindly admit that there is a *here* and an *elsewhere;* every artifice of seduction and the marching dawn are at stake): we Westerners have already stopped belonging to ourselves, and in vain do we try to conjure you up, adorable scourge, all-too-uncertain deliverance! In our cities, the avenues, running parallel from North to South, all converge in a no man's land made of our blasé detective gazes. As for *who* might have handed us this insoluble case, we haven't a clue. Revelation, the right not to think and act as a herd, our only remaining chance to rediscover our reason: throughout our dream, these leave behind only a hand clenched save for the index finger, which imperiously designates a spot on the horizon. There, the light and air begin in all purity to proudly erect thoughts yet unformed. Man restored to his primordial sovereignty and serenity preaches there, they say, for himself alone, the eternal truth of himself alone. He has no notion of the hideous orchestration that has made us its final victims; of the key reality that prevents us from moving. Once again, we should not leave, for that man has no choice but to come meet us: he is coming, he has already converted the best among us.

Orient, victorious Orient, you who have but a symbolic value, do with me as you will, pearl-colored Orient! In the flow of a sentence as much as in the mysterious wind of a jazz tune, let me recognize your projects for the coming Revolutions. You, the dazzling image of my dispossession, Orient, beautiful bird of prey and innocence, I implore you from the depths of this realm of shadows! Inspire me, so that I may be the one who no longer has a shadow.

September 1924

Burial Denied

IF IT WAS ALREADY BEHIND the times to speak of Anatole France while he was alive, let's at least give a grateful nod to the newspaper that's carrying him off, the wicked daily that had brought him forth. Loti, Barrès, France: all things considered, we should mark in beautiful white the year that put down those three sinister clowns: the idiot, the traitor, and the cop. We should – no objections from me – reserve a special word of scorn for the latter. With France, we're losing a bit of human servility. They should declare a national holiday to commemorate the end of his craftiness, traditionalism, patriotism, opportunism, skepticism, realism, and coldness! Let's not forget that the vilest hypocrites of our time claimed Anatole France as an accomplice and let's never forgive him for having draped his smiling inertia in the colors of the Revolution. To bury his corpse, someone ought to dump the old books "he loved so well" from one of those stalls along the quays, stuff him inside, and toss the whole thing into the Seine. Now that he's dead, the man mustn't be allowed to shed any more dust.

October 1924

In Self-Defense

FROM WITHOUT TO WITHIN, from within to without, as Surrealists we continue to honor only that *summons* which we consider total and unparalleled, by virtue of which we are appointed to give and receive what no one before us has given or received; we continue to preside over a kind of vertiginous exchange, without which we would lose all interest in the meaning of our lives – whether through laziness or rage, or by giving in to our own weakness. This weakness is a fact: it has kept us from playing our part in numerous situations, even when our ideas on the matter at hand were not shared by anyone else. We are well aware that at a higher level of expression (namely, action), such ideas would put us outside the law. Without wishing to shock anyone – that is, without really caring whether we do or not – we consider Mr. Poincaré's presence at the head of the French government a serious obstacle to intelligence, a somewhat gratuitous insult to *the mind,* a vicious joke that we should not let stand. We know, moreover, that we are not likely to curry favor with the liberal opinion of our times, and it should be understood that we could truly applaud Mr. Poincaré's disappearance only if most of his political opponents followed suit. Still, it's true that the man's traits alone are reason enough for our disgust. The sinister "Lorraine" is already an old acquaintance of ours: we were twenty years old. Without indulging in personal vendettas, and while refusing to hang our every anxiety on the social conditions forced upon us, we are constantly obliged to look back, and to hate.

Nonetheless, our situation in the modern world is such that

our embrace of a program like the Communist one – an enthusiastic embrace in principle, though naturally we consider this program to be strictly minimal* – has been greeted only with great suspicion, as if this embrace were ultimately deemed unacceptable. As we had no intention whatsoever of criticizing the French Communist Party (given our faith in the Revolution, this would have been inconsistent with our ways of thinking), we must protest so unjust a sentence. The fact is that for more than a year our overtures have run up against a muted hostility that has taken every opportunity to show itself. And given this, I see no reason to abstain any longer from saying that *L'Humanité* – puerile, bombastic, needlessly *cretinizing* – is unreadable as a newspaper and completely worthless in its self-appointed role as educator to the masses. Behind those quickly scanned articles, which focus so tightly on current events that they leave no room for the larger picture, which scream at the top of their lungs about specifics,

---

* Let me explain. We do not have the impertinence to counter the Communist program with one of our own. As it stands, this program is the only one that seems to be viably inspired by the circumstances, that has based its goals once and for all on its overall chances of success, and that presents in both its theoretical development and its execution all the earmarks of inevitability. Outside of this program, we find only empiricism and daydreams. And yet, there are certain gaps that all our hopes in Communism's ultimate triumph cannot fill: isn't man implacably the enemy of his fellow man? won't boredom end only when the world does? aren't any assurances about life and honor vain? etc. How can one avoid the occurrence of these questions, and consequently a particular frame of mind, which we would be hard pressed not to take into account? This frame of mind is rather seductive, and discussions of economic factors by men who are not specialists in the field (and who by nature are not likely to specialize in anything) aren't enough to preserve us from it. If it is of paramount importance that we renounce and abandon the issue, then so be it. If not, we will continue despite ourselves to have reservations about completely embracing a faith that, like any other, presupposes a certain state of grace.

which present Russia's admirable difficulties as so many insane joyrides, which discourage any extrapolitical activities other than sports, which glorify unsatisfying jobs, and which heap abuse on common-law prisoners, it is impossible not to sense an extreme weariness on the part of those who foist them on us, a secret resignation to what exists, as well as a desire to keep the reader in a state of generous illusion – and with the least possible effort to boot. Understand that I am speaking technically, looking strictly at the overall effectiveness of a given text or group of texts. To my mind, nothing here seems to live up to the intended effect, either on the surface or in depth.* Nor do I see any real effort, other than the constant reminder of immediate human interests – any effort that might keep the mind away from things unrelated to the search for its fundamental necessity (and we can establish that this necessity can only be the Revolution) – any more than I see a serious attempt to dissipate what are often superficial quarrels, bearing only on specific methods that, were it not for the division into camps whose goals we in no way oppose, could scarcely imperil the cause we're defending.**

I cannot comprehend how on the road to revolt there can be a right and a left. As to the gratification of immediate human interests – apparently the only motive worth imputing to revolutionary action these days† – let me simply add that I see more

---

* I'll make an exception for the contributions of Jacques Doriot, Camille Fégy, Marcel Fourrier, and Victor Crastre, which inspire total confidence.

** I believe in the possibility of reconciling to some extent with the anarchists, rather than with the Socialists; and I believe in the need to forgive certain figures of the first rank (such as Boris Souvarine) their character flaws.

† I repeat that many revolutionaries, of various tendencies, imagine no other motives. According to Marcel Martinet (in the May 15 issue of *Europe*), the Surrealists' dissatisfaction arose only after the war, because they were *hurting in*

drawbacks than benefits in exploiting it. It seems to me that the class instinct stands to lose by it everything that the instinct of self-preservation, in the most mediocre sense, stands to win. The material advantages a man might hope to gain from the Revolution are hardly enough to make him gamble his life – his life – on the red card. He would still need compelling reasons to sacrifice the little he has for the nothing he might get in return. We know these reasons; they are our own. I believe they are the same for every revolutionary. An account of them would shed a different light, inspire a different confidence from the ones that the Communist press would like to inculcate in us. Far be it from me to try to distract the attention that the heads of the French Communist Party are seeking to draw to current problems: I will limit myself to denouncing the errors of a propaganda method that strikes me as deplorable. If you ask me, any effort to revise these methods could not be too great or too soon.

It is without presumption, but by the same token without timidity, that I make these few observations. Even from the Marxist point of view, they could not reasonably be denied. The activities of *L'Humanité* are far from blameless. What one reads in it is not always liable to hold one's attention nor *a fortiori* to attract it. The true currents of modern thought show up in its pages less often than anywhere else. In these pages, the life of the mind is practically nil. Everything revolves around vague grievances, idle denigration, petty disputes. Here and there we can spot a more pronounced symptom of impotence: one writer does

the pocketbook. "If the Krauts had paid up, there would have been no dissatisfaction, and the question of Revolution would not have arisen any more than after a strike that brings a few cents more pay." A statement for which we leave him the responsibility, and whose obvious bad faith absolves me from having to answer his article point for point.

nothing but string quotations together, another hides behind authorities, and sometimes they even rehabilitate traitors such as Guesde and Vaillant.* Must we at all costs let this pass in silence? To what end?

I say that the revolutionary flame burns where it will, and that it is not up to a small group of individuals, *in this period of antic-ipation we're living through,* to decree that it can burn only here or there. One needs to be quite sure of oneself to make such a deter-mination, and the least we can say is that *L'Humanité,* caught up as it is in these various exclusions, is not always the beautiful flaming broadside that we'd like to have in our hands.

Among the offers of help it receives and spurns (because of I don't know what narrow-mindedness), thereby remaining the all-but-unintelligible echo of Moscow's great voice, there is not one – not even ours, special as our services might be – that isn't made wholeheartedly. Let me say a few words about that. If our con-tribution to revolutionary action in this regard were to be accept-ed, we would be the last to try to overstep its limits, which relate to our specific abilities. Perhaps it's not asking too much not to be dismissed as a negligible quantity. If anyone today has the right to wield a pen, without bringing to it the slightest professional vanity, and only because they alone have banished chance from the written word – all chance, good and bad luck, profit and loss – I believe it is us, who moreover hardly write at all anymore; and we leave it to individuals who are even *freer* than we are to eval-uate this someday. For me, in 1926, there was nothing to be done, not even to answer this letter from Henri Barbusse:

* Jules Guesde, one of the first to introduce Marxism to France, and Edouard Vaillant, an early member of the Communist International, both adopted ultra-conservative, nationalist positions during World War I. [*trans.*]

Dear colleague,

I have assumed literary editorship of the newspaper *L'Humanité*. We would like to make it into a great voice of the people, with its actions exerted in every major sphere of contemporary activity and thought.

L'Humanité will notably publish a new short story every day. I am asking if you would agree in principle to contribute something to this section of our newspaper.

Furthermore, I would be grateful if you could submit proposals and ideas for press campaigns that would be in keeping with a large-circulation proletarian newspaper intended to enlighten and instruct the masses, to further the indictment that has become imperative against reactionary tendencies, insufficiencies, abuses, and perversions of current "culture," and to pave the way for a great human and collective art that seems to us increasingly imperative in these times of ours.

With the best will in the world, I cannot give Mr. Barbusse what he is asking for. I would probably yield to the desire to submit proposals and ideas for press campaigns to *L'Humanité* if I weren't entirely dissuaded by the idea of Mr. Barbusse as its literary editor. Mr. Barbusse once wrote a perfectly respectable book called *Under Fire*. To tell the truth, it was more like a long newspaper article, of undeniable informational value, which reestablished in their elementary veracity a series of facts that many people at the time were eager to mask or distort. It was basically a passable documentary, though not as effective as one reel of actual film showing scenes of carnage under the amused eye of the *same* Mr. Poincaré, the sight of which has thus far been denied us. The little I know about Mr. Barbusse's literary production, moreover, only confirms my sense that if the overnight success of

Under Fire hadn't taken him by surprise and made him the tributary of the violent hopes of thousands of men who expected, almost demanded, that he become their spokesman, nothing would have designated him as the soul of the masses, *the projector*. Nor, intellectually speaking, is he – as are the writers whom we Surrealists have made a profession of admiring – *an enlightener*. Mr. Barbusse is, if not a reactionary, at least a latecomer, which is perhaps no better. Not only is he incapable of externalizing, as Zola did, whatever feelings he might have about the public ill and of making even delicate skins feel the horrible wind of poverty, but he does not even participate in any way in the internal drama that for several years has been playing out among a few men – whose outcome, as might one day be recognized, affects all men. As far as I'm concerned, the importance I attach to this latter endeavor and the emotion it inspires in me do not afford me the leisure of publishing "short stories," not even in *L'Humanité*. I have never written short stories, having neither my own nor others' time to waste. To me, it's an outdated genre, and I don't need to explain that I am judging not according to fashion, but by virtue of the overall meaning of the questions I ask myself. These days, anyone who wants to write or read a "short story" would have to be a pretty pathetic sap. Whether Mr. Barbusse likes it or not, sentimental inanity has had its day. Outside of any literary rubric, the only "stories" that we can admit, that we might know of, are the news stories that *L'Humanité* provides of the revolutionary situation, when it takes the trouble not to copy them from rival newspapers. Mr. Barbusse and his henchmen cannot plunge us back into vague melancholy.

It goes without saying that Mr. Barbusse makes easy prey. Still, here is a man who, on the same plane where we operate, enjoys a credit that nothing valid can justify: he is neither a man of action, nor a spiritual guide, nor absolutely anything at all. On the pretext that his latest novel (called *Chains,* apparently) earned him a few threatening letters, he whines in the September 1 and September 9 issues of *L'Humanité* about the thanklessness of his task, the difficulties of his relations with the proletarian public, "the only public whose readership counts," to which he is "deeply attached," etc., etc. This done, he then proceeds, "with respect to words, the raw materials of style," to awkwardly reopen a debate about which we would have much to say and in which we see no place for him:

> In last week's article, I described the strong current of stylistic renewal that is now becoming visible and that seemed to me worth qualifying as revolutionary. I endeavored to show that this renewal, which unfortunately* remains only on the level of form in the superficial domain of means of expression [?], is modifying every aspect of literature.

What does this mean? While we have never ceased taking infinite precautions to remain masters of our research, just about anyone could come along, with confusionistic intentions that I understand only too well, and liken our attitudes – and above all the attitudes of men such as Lautréamont, for example – to those of the motley crew of professional scribblers with whom Henri Barbusse is trying to make friends! Let me quote several lines from the August 1 issue of the *Bulletin de la Vie artistique:*

* That "unfortunately" is a poem unto itself.

Surrealist activity as a whole cannot be boiled down to mere automatism. The Surrealists use writing in an entirely voluntary way, in contradiction with their feelings toward this automatism, and toward ends that I don't have room to examine here. Let us simply note that their actions and their painting (which is situated along the same lines) belong to the vast enterprise of recreating the universe to which Lautréamont and Lenin completely devoted themselves.

I don't think this could have been put any better, and in no way is the juxtaposition of the two names mentioned in the last sentence arbitrary or whimsical. As we see it, those two names cannot be set in opposition, and we hope mightily to make people understand why. Mr. Barbusse should pay attention, which would keep him from abusing the workers' trust by praising the works of Paul Claudel and Cocteau, authors of infamous patriotic poems and nauseating Catholic professions of faith, ignominious profiteers of the regime and arrant counter-revolutionaries. They are, he says, "innovators" – something no one would ever dream of saying about Mr. Barbusse, the famous old bore. It's bad enough that he sees Jules Supervielle and Luc Durtain, with the greatest authority and value, as representative of the latest tendencies: you know, Jules Supervielle and Luc Durtain, those "two writers so remarkable as writers" (*sic*) – but Cocteau, but Claudel! And why not, apropos the next monument to the dead, an impartial defense of Mr. Poincaré's *talent* by a political columnist from *L'Humanité?* If Mr. Barbusse weren't a fraud of the worst sort, he would not make a show of believing that a work's revolutionary value and its seeming originality are one and the same. I say "seeming originality," for any attempt to isolate the originality of the works in question would only point up Mr.

Barbusse's ignorance. Let me be clear that the publication in *L'Humanité* of the article "On Words, the Raw Materials of Style" stands for me as a *sign of the times* and deserves to be highlighted as such. One could not do a worse job, in passing (and I do mean in passing), than Mr. Barbusse.

We have always said and we maintain that the emancipation of style, which could be realized up to a certain point in bourgeois society, cannot consist in laboratory experiments abstractly focusing on words. In this domain as in any other, we believe that only revolt is creative, and that is why we consider every kind of revolt worthwhile. Hugo's most beautiful lines were written by an implacable enemy of oppression; Borel, in the portrait that adorns one of his books, holds a dagger in his hand; Rabbe considered himself "a supernumerary of life"; Baudelaire cursed God, and Rimbaud vowed not to be of this world. There can be no salvation for their works apart from this. It is only by knowing this that we can consider their debt to us *paid in full*. But as for letting ourselves be duped by what today passes itself off as the external equivalent of these works without possessing any of their substance: never. For it is indeed a matter of "substance," even in the philosophical sense of realized necessity. Only the realization of a necessity is revolutionary in nature. Therefore, we must not say that a work is revolutionary in its essence unless – contrary to those works that Mr. Barbusse recommends – its "substance" can support the claim.

Only then can one look to words, and to the more or less radical ways of treating them. The fact is, this treatment is usually unwitting – for those who have something to say, at least – and one would have to be the basest simpleton to pay any attention to the Futurist theory of "words in liberty," based as it is on an infantile belief in the real and independent existence of words.

One might even say that this theory is a striking example of what the desire to resemble one's greatest and proudest precursors can suggest to a man in love only with novelty. Everyone knows that against this theory, as against many others no less precarious, we have set automatic writing, which introduces into the problem an element that hasn't been sufficiently explored but, at the same time, prevents the problem itself from being posed.

Still, until this problem is no longer raised at all, we will continue to prevent its pure and simple avoidance. For us, the issue is not to revive words and subject them to clever manipulations in the hope of forging a new style, interesting as it might be. To posit that words are the raw materials of style is hardly more ingenious than introducing letters as the basis of the alphabet. Words are, in fact, something else entirely, and they might even be *everything*. We pity those who have understood only the literary uses to which they can be put and who boast of paving the way for "the artistic renaissance that the social renaissance of tomorrow is calling for and sketching out." What should we care about that artistic renaissance? Long live the social Revolution, and it alone! We have too serious a bone to pick with the mind, we live too uneasily in our thoughts, we suffer too painfully the burden of those "styles" dear to Mr. Barbusse to devote even the slightest attention to anything else.

Once again, all we know is that we have a certain gift for words and that, because of this, something great and obscure tends imperiously to be expressed through us; that each of us was chosen and designated to himself from among a thousand others to formulate what, in our lifetimes, must be formulated. This is an order that we have received once and for all and that we have never had the luxury of disputing. It might seem to us – paradoxical though this might be – that what we're saying is not what most needs to be said, and that there might be better ways of saying it. But it's as if we had been condemned to it for all eternity. As I see it, to write – I mean to write with such difficulty, and not in order to seduce or, in its usual sense, to live, but at most to be morally self-sufficient, without being able to remain deaf to a singular and tireless call – to write in this way is neither to play nor to cheat. Perhaps our task is only to liquidate a spiritual legacy that it would be in everyone's interest to renounce, and no more.

We seriously deplore the fact that the complete perversion of western culture in our time makes it impossible for anyone speaking with a modicum of rigor to be heard by most of his intended audience. It would seem that everything keeps these two sides from meeting. That which is thought (merely for the glory of being thought) has become almost incomprehensible to the masses and is all but untranslatable for them. It has even been said that one must be "initiated" in order to understand certain texts. And yet, it is still a matter of life and death, of love and reason, of justice and crime. There can be no disinterested parties!

This is where the entire meaning of my present critique resides. I humbly repeat, I do not know how anyone today can hope to reduce the desperate misunderstanding stemming from the apparently insurmountable difficulties in objectifying ideas. On our own initiative, we placed ourselves at the center of this misunderstanding and vowed to ensure that it wouldn't worsen. From a strictly revolutionary viewpoint, reading *L'Humanité* would tend to confirm our fears. In placing ourselves there, we thought we were fulfilling our roles by denouncing the most characteristic impostures and deviations around us, and we also believed that, having nothing to gain by standing squarely on the political terrain, we could rightfully hearken back to certain basic principles of human activity and thereby serve as best we could the cause of the Revolution.

The French Communist Party has constantly and openly denigrated our attitude, and even the author of a recent pamphlet called *La Révolution et les Intellectuels: Que peuvent faire les Surréalistes?** who tries to define it in Marxist terms with complete impartiality, has accused us of vacillating between Marxism and anarchy and basically called upon us to choose. Here, moreover, is his essential question to us: "Yes or no, is this desired revolution *a priori* that of the mind, or that of the factual world? Is it linked to Marxism or to contemplative theories, to the purification of inner life?" The question is much more subtle than it appears, although its principal malice seems to me to reside in the opposition between inner reality and the factual world, a wholly artificial opposition that does not bear up under scrutiny. In the realm of facts, as far as we're concerned there can be no doubt: there is not one of us who does not hope for the passage of power from the hands of the bourgeoisie to those of the proletariat. In the meantime, we deem it absolutely necessary that inner life should pursue its experiments, and this, of course, without external control, not even Marxist. Doesn't Surrealism, moreover, tend to posit these two states as essentially one and the same, refuting their supposed irreconcilability by every means possible – beginning with the most primitive means of all, the use of which we would otherwise be hard put to defend: I mean the appeal to the marvelous?**

---

* Pierre Naville. [*trans.*]

** The limits of the present study will not allow me to dwell at length on this subject. Do I still need to demonstrate that Surrealism has taken no other goal for itself? It is time, as we vehemently continue to affirm, more than ever it is

But so long as the fusion of these two states remains purely ideal, so long as one cannot say to what extent it will finally come about (for the moment, we can only state that it is conceivable), there is no need to put us in contradiction with ourselves with respect to the meanings we might give certain words, certain *buffer words*, such as the word "Orient." This word – which plays, as do so many others, on a literal meaning and several figurative ones, as well as on various misinterpretations – has been used more and more frequently in recent years. It must correspond to a particular concern of our era, to its most secret hope, to an unconscious anticipation; it cannot be recurring with such insistence merely in vain. In itself, it constitutes an argument as valid as any other, and today's reactionaries know it well, they who waste no opportunity to challenge anything Oriental.

"Too many signs," writes Massis, "make us fear that these pseudo-Oriental doctrines, enlisted in the service of disorder, finally serve only to revive the dissents that, since the reformation, have fallen onto the spirit of Europe, and that *Asiaticism*, like the *Germanism* of earlier times, is but the first message of the

---

time for the mind to revise certain purely formal oppositions of terms, such as the opposition between word and action, between dream and reality, between the present, the past, and the future. The soundness of these distinctions, in the deplorable conditions of existence in Europe at the beginning of the twentieth century, even from a practical viewpoint, can no longer be defended for an instant. Why not mobilize all the resources of the imagination to remedy it? If, with us, poetry wins out: so much the better or the worse, but that's not the issue. We stand wholeheartedly with Count Hermann Keyserling, on the path toward a *monotonous* metaphysics. "They speak always only of the One, without a second, in which God, soul, and the world flow together, the One which is the innermost essence of all multiplicity. Indian metaphysics too refer to something purely intensive. They refer to life itself, that ultimate, essentially unobjective Reality from which objects are poured forth like sudden fancies."

Barbarians." Valéry insinuates that "the Greeks and Romans showed us how to deal with the Asian monsters." He's speaking as a stomach: "Moreover, the issue in such matters is one of *digestion.*" For Maurras, Albert Gareau tells us, all unreason comes from the disruptive powers of the East. "All the great catastrophes of our history, all the great dissents can be interpreted by the heat of the same Jewish and Syrian miasma, by the bitter folly of the Orient and its sensitive religion and its taste for storms that it offers to tired minds." Given this, why shouldn't we continue being inspired by the Orient, or even by the "pseudo-Orient," to which Surrealism gladly serves as a mere homage, the way the eye studies a pearl? Tagore, one of those wicked Oriental thinkers, believes that "Western civilization can avoid perishing if it immediately begins seeking the harmony that it shattered for the benefit of its material nature." Between us, it's patently impossible, and there goes a doomed civilization. What we can't abide, I say, and this is the entire point of the present article, is that man should hope to restore his equilibrium – shattered in the West, it's true, for the benefit of his material nature – by making still more sacrifices to his material nature. And yet, in all good faith, this is what certain revolutionaries think, notably within the French Communist Party. There exists a moral domain where like does not cure like, where homeopathy is worthless. It is not through "mechanization" that Western populations can be saved, however widespread the watchword *electrification* might be; that is not how they will escape the moral ill that is killing them. I completely agree with the author of *La Révolution et les Intellectuels* that "the wage system is a material necessity to which three-quarters of the world's population are bound, independent of the philosophical concepts of so-called Westerners or Easterners" and that "under the yoke of capital both sides are exploited"; but I cannot share his conclusion, to wit that "intellectual quarrels are absolutely vain given the unity of this condition." I believe, on the contrary, that man should abandon his powers of discrimination less than ever; that in this domain doctrinaire Surrealism would indeed be out of place; and that under deeper scrutiny, which should be attempted, the *wage system* would not pass for the effective cause of the situation we are suffering – that man would accept another cause for himself, which human intelligence, and our intelligence in particular, has every right to seek out.*

We must complain of having met some serious obstacles in this regard. If we were suspected of passivity vis-à-vis the various undertakings of capitalist banditry, that would be one thing, but it isn't even the case. Nothing in the world would make us defend an inch of French soil, but we would defend to the death, in Russia or in China, a minuscule conquest by the proletariat. Since we are here, we hope to perform our revolutionary duty on this soil as we would anywhere else. We might lack a political turn of mind, but at least no one can accuse us of living enclosed

---

* I have no intention of challenging *historical materialism* but rather materialism, period. Is it really necessary to recall that, in the minds of Marx and Engels, the former came about only as the desired and definitive negation of the latter? There can be no confusion on this subject. As we see it, the idea of historical materialism, whose ingenious character we wouldn't dream of contradicting, can sustain itself (and, more importantly, ultimately be exalted) and make us envision its consequences concretely only if it regains awareness of itself at every moment, if it fearlessly stands up to all antagonistic ideas – beginning with the ones it initially had to overcome in order to exist, which tend to crop up again in new forms. As we see it, these latter ideas seem to be making their underhanded way into the minds of certain French Communist Party leaders. May we ask them to meditate on Théodore Jouffroy's terrible pages in *Comment les dogmes finissent?*

in our thoughts, as if in some tower while others are trading gunfire down below. With all our hearts, we have always refused to enter that tower, and we will not allow others to shut us up in it. Perhaps indeed our attempted cooperation with the liveliest elements of the "Clarté" group in the winter of 1925–26, in view of some well-defined external action, ended in a practical failure; but if we could not reach an agreement, it was emphatically *not* because of our "inability to resolve the fundamental antinomy that exists in Surrealist thinking." I believe I've made it clear that this antinomy does not exist. The only thing we ran up against, on both sides, was our fear of acting against the true designs of the Communist International and the impossibility of trying to "know only the orders" (disconcerting, to say the least) given by the French party. That is essentially why *La Guerre civile* never appeared.*

How can one avoid begging the question? Only recently I was again told, in full knowledge of the facts, that I committed an error in this article by attacking, from outside the Party, the editor of one of its periodicals; and once again they explained that this action – as well-intentioned and praiseworthy as it might seem – would merely provide ammunition to the enemies of a Party that I myself believe is, in revolutionary terms, the only force we can count on. This had not escaped me, and I admit that it's the reason why I hesitated to speak for so long, and why I finally decided to do so only reluctantly. And it is true, absolutely true, that such a discussion, which in no way aims at weaken-

* Breton is referring to the Surrealists' attempted fusion with the proto-Communist group "Clarté," which resulted in various practical resolutions outside of the Communist Party structure, and which would have published its activities in a joint magazine called *La Guerre civile*. As he notes, both the project and the magazine collapsed before they ever got off the ground. [*trans.*]

ing the Party, should have taken place within the Party itself. But as its own members admitted, they would have cut this discussion as short as possible, assuming they would have let it begin at all. For myself and those who think as I do, there was nothing to expect from such a discussion. In this regard, I knew as of last year what I could hope for, and that is why I deemed it pointless to *join* the Communist Party. I do not wish to be arbitrarily thrown back into the "opposition" against a party to which, on every other point, I adhere with all my might. But since it has Reason on its side, I do think that the Party, if it were better led, if it were truly itself, should have all the answers to the questions I've raised.

I will conclude by adding that, despite everything, I am still waiting for such an answer. I am not about to join the other side. I only hope that the absence of a large number of individuals such as myself, held back for equally valid reasons, does not thin the ranks of those who are usefully and consciously paving the way for the proletarian Revolution – especially if into these ranks slip phantoms, in other words creatures whose true nature they do not see and who want no part of that Revolution.

. . . .

Self-defense?

December 1926

Paul Eluard's Capital of Pain

U PON A THOUSAND LINES of dots that we cannot see, Paul Eluard's great book *Capital of Pain* opens and shuts. Whatever we may think, dear friends, what could have taken place, and what might still take place? To be or not to be – we are just beginning to see that *that* is not the question. And this is probably the first work that isn't essentially built around this false and persistent dilemma.

Capital of Pain is written for those people who are proud of (or are concealing) the fact that, for a long time, they haven't felt like reading anything: either because they soon exhausted what they could get from reading, refusing on principle to sanction *literary games;* or because they were pursuing some obsession, idea, or entity from which they could not be diverted and that no one else could approach; or else because, for some entirely different reason, at this particular time in their life, they wanted to sacrifice the faculty of learning to the power of forgetting. The miracle of this poetry is that it mingles all these secrets into a single secret – Eluard's – that now takes on the colors of eternity.

Even as this collection not only withstands but in fact encourages the loftiest comparisons – even as in its light, as in no other, action and contemplation end their struggle, human torment stops arousing pity, and things dreamed cease to pose a threat to things that *are* – more wonderful still is the choice that Paul Eluard imposes on us all, the marvel of the words he assembles, the order in which he assembles them: a choice that works through him rather than one he works through. As his friend, I would hold it against myself if I didn't praise, simply and without reservation, the vast, strange, rapid, profound, splendid, and distressing *movements of his heart.*

Capital of Pain: apparently it scandalizes certain people when passion and inspiration realize they need nothing other than themselves.

1926

The X..., Y... Exhibit

ALTHOUGH I DO NOT BELIEVE in madness, during the war I knew a madman who didn't believe in the war. As he saw it, the so-called "hostilities" were simply the magnified image of a torture inflicted on him, without his knowing why (but many of us were in the same boat).

He lost not a single detail of the stage set from those days. Although he came from the front, nothing made much of an impression on him: you think you're stepping over cadavers, but what if they'd been put there before the bombings, or even if they were made of wax? why should the risk of infection keep you from looking for the wound, verifying the existence of the wound under the bandage?

Looking at X...'s paintings, I thought once more of this state of perfect incredulity we must be in, because the more it goes on, the more it engages our capacity for illusion. I recognize it in this bandaged head. We have to recognize our growing ingratitude toward life. From all the gaping aspects of the world that we have to deal with, one by one, let creatures emerge who doubt wildly, who can constantly test our ability to resist what passes for being, and to render more or less impossible what is not. There is...there is a mask covering all the faces we think we see most clearly: each landscape finds us in the same expectant pose, as if watching a curtain rise, and I am speaking only as a reminder of the human poses dreamed by plants, the mandrake root, the daphne. I mention only in passing the dizzying, mechanical, and mysterious mobility of hands, the fistfuls of moths they scatter into the air; these hands lead up to stems we can't see, alight on wrecked telephone lines, circle around innumerable objects that are the color of time. These are the objects that a painter might be tempted to show us today, instead of others. What, again, is this visual field sadly lit by physical considerations and outside of which no element of the canvas has been considered – as if one could say that our attention is drawn equally by all the windows in those houses, all the folds in that dress; that our interest is sufficiently roused by the absurd copy of what we are not even thinking of looking at (and vulgar distortion is not what will manage to legitimize these practices in my eyes)? What is this visual field next to the other, whose ceaseless exhibition hardly suffers from the texture or arrangement of a sensitive organ like the human eye, stupid when compared to that of a chameleon, and especially to the *eyes behind the eyes,* of which little Cornelius, Achim von Arnim's adorable character, was so justly proud? This field, I was saying, where there appears (according to the least prevalent psychic laws) the substance of human thought delivered to its spirits and personal demons, hidden in the bushes, variously erratic, multiply intentional without knowing it, deceiving the social beast in spite of itself and sheltering – while speaking, alone or not, of the hour or the creature it loves, in other places and times, on equal footing – guests that are no more commonly found together than Henrietta of England, the shadow of an immense horsetail, and a bobbin of a waspwaist?

It is absolutely essential to say this: the time of Baudelairean correspondences (which have become an odious critical commonplace) is over. Personally, I refuse to see them as anything but the expression of a transitional and frankly rather timid idea, which, given the poetic and pictorial efforts being made today, no longer has anything to say about anything. Oneiric values have definitely won out over the others, and I maintain that anyone who still refuses to *see,* for instance, a horse galloping on a tomato, must be an idiot. A tomato is also a child's balloon – Surrealism, again, having suppressed the word "like." The horse is about to merge with the cloud, etc. So what? Well, all right, what would you say if a few of us, very sure of ourselves, piled into one of those old jalopies from the Mack Sennett comedies, where you could see the world through the eyes of Y..., truly as if from nowhere?

The sky is a lovely bowl of faded stars, and it is admirable to see how for a woman endowed with violence everything within her reach is charged with supreme reasons; how she can turn aside even the river of images if called upon to protect spiritually her beaver village. It's with a certain emotion that I see her keeping watch in the corners of those intentionally disturbing canvasses, over everything that might resemble the maintenance of birds' nests in the lightning-struck trees, over the preservation of what, like Rimbaud's prayer to the rainbow, must come after the Flood – after the Flood coming after and with us. Let man today deny without reservation anything that can weigh him down and subject him; let him die if need be on a barricade of flowers, if only to give substance to a chimera, to a woman, perhaps, the only one who can save both what she carries and what carries her away – silence! There is no solution outside of love.

April 1929

Notice to the Reader of
The Hundred Headless Woman

THE SPLENDID ILLUSTRATIONS of popular novels and children's books, such as *Rocambole* or *Costal the Indian,* dedicated to those who can barely read, are among the few things that can move to tears those who claim to have read everything. The path of knowledge, which increasingly tends to replace astonishing virgin forests with the most depressing deserts, lacking even the slightest mirage, is not the kind that allows for retreat. At most, we can secretly open the same gilt-edged volume, or one of those dog-eared books (as if we needed only to find the magician's hat), whose shining or somber pages, perhaps more than anything, determined the particular nature of our dreams, the elective reality of our love, and the incomparable development of our life. And if that is how a soul is formed, what can we expect of a common and simple soul that fashions itself every day on images rather than texts, that needs to be brutally shocked by the sight of blood, the black and white ceremonials, the ninety-degree angle of spring, the shabby miracles, the endless refrains; of an utterly candid soul that simultaneously vibrates in millions of men and that, in the bright revolutionary daylight, because it is simple and candid, will carve out its own veritable emblems in the unchanged colors of its exaltation? These colors, which are all we wish to retain from hymns, golden vessels, volleys of bullets, dazzling feathers, and flags, even if they are missing from the illustrations that shine like showers of sparks above a distant, suspended sentence ("Shoking cried out: 'Peace, Sultan'"; or, "His half-open cloak revealed a lantern hung from his neck"; or, "They all went for their swords at the same moment"), a sentence awakening the ever more mysterious echoes (and who knows why?) of the *passé défini*, are the ones that willy-nilly, from birth to death, tint our enchantment and terror. Language, whether written or spoken, is powerless to describe the furtive and extremely suggestive motions of animate or inanimate beings within an event, and it is quite obvious that one can show nothing of a character in whom we're trying to be interested unless one draws his portrait. Given all this, how could we not deplore that so far only flat adventure stories have benefited from any true deepening in the sense we mean, and that, on top of this, most of the artists assigned to provide visible value to what would otherwise remain rather spectral have not hesitated to turn attention away from what *happens,* by authorial will, and to focus it instead on their "style"? Yet it is only their complete and willing subordination to the slightest whims of the text, their enthusiastic abandon to the highest tone a work can reach, that today proclaim the genius of the anonymous illustrator of the *Chronicles of Duke Ernst,* so dear to Max Ernst, and the man who created the covers of *Fantômas.*

It remains for us to study these pages, ornamented like so many ironwork grills, detaching themselves from a thousand ancient books that can no longer be justified, I mean that can no longer be recommended as reading on any possible grounds; these drawn pages that, separated from other deadly pages to which they refer, represent for us a sum of conjectures so misleading that they become precious, like the incredibly precise reconstitution of the scene of a crime that we might witness in our dreams, without caring in the least about the killers or motives. Many of these pages, displaying an agitation all the more extraordinary in that its pretext escapes us – as is the case with pages from any technical work, provided it treats nothing familiar to us – give us the illusion of actual cuts made in time, space, customs, and even beliefs. There is not a single element that isn't hazardous; not one that, to satisfy the elastic conditions of probability, we might be forbidden to use for any other purpose. That white-bearded man coming out of a house with a lantern: if I cover what he is lighting, he might just as well be standing near a winged lion; if I hide his lantern, his hands, in that position, could be scattering stars or stones on the ground. Superposition, moreover, without my noticing it, and even so long as I don't notice it, works, if not exactly before our eyes, at least very objectively and continuously. A marvelous arrangement, which *skips over the pages* like a little girl jumping rope, or drawing a magic ring to use as a hoop, circles the storehouse day and night, the storehouse where the things we involuntarily bother to consider or retain pile up in total chaos. The truth specific to each of us is a game of solitaire whose elements we have to seize on the fly, without ever having seen them before.

Everything that has been thought, described, given as false, dubious or certain, but above all depicted, has a singular power of disturbance over us: it is clear that it can't be *possessed,* and so it becomes all the more impatiently desired. The most knowledgeable of men will almost constantly take pleasure in some "exalted learning," as if in the frantic, fleeting images in a wood fire. History itself, with the childish impressions it leaves in our minds – obscurely those of Charles VI and Geneviève de Brabant rather than of Mary Stuart and Louis XIV – falls *outside* like snow.

We were waiting for a book that would mainly stress the inevitable accentuation of certain lines, brought out by the erasure of all the others; a book whose author could leap over the breach of uninterest that makes it less interesting to ponder a statue in a square than in a ditch, or that makes an aurora borealis less lovely when reproduced in the magazine *La Nature* than anywhere else. Surreality will depend on our will toward complete disorientation from everything (and it goes without saying that you can disorient a hand by isolating it from its arm, that this hand takes on more value as a hand, and also that when speaking of disorientation, we are not thinking only about its spatial possibilities). We were waiting for a book that would avoid the trap of trying to bear no resemblance to any other book except ink and print – as if, to make a statue appear in a ditch, you had to be the maker of that statue. Let me add, moreover, that for this statue to be really disoriented, it must first have lived a conventional life, in its conventional place. I believe the entire value of such an enterprise – and perhaps of any artistic enterprise – depends on taste, daring, and success from having secured for oneself certain *amusements*. And we were waiting for a book that would spell out simultaneously the mysterious, disturbing qualities of several universes that mingle only through a physico-moral postulate that strikes us as infinitely *mediocre* and at the very least undesirably insignificant (take a bottle: *they* think right off that we are going to drink, but no, it is empty, corked, and bobbing about on the water; oh, *they* get it, the bottle in the ocean, and so on). Things are called upon to do something other than what's usually expected. In fact, it's by consciously forgoing their primary function (manipulating for the first time an object whose use or former use you don't know) that certain transcendent properties can be deduced, which attach to these things in another conceived or conceivable world where, for example, a hatchet can be taken for a sunset; where the appreciation of virtual elements is no longer allowed (I imagine a ghost, at the crossing of several roads, busy reading a signpost); where the faculty of migration, left only to birds, also takes hold of autumn leaves; where past, present, and future lives join in one life which is *life,* utterly depersonalized as it is. (Too bad for painters: never using their imagination to do more than make one or two heads. And novelists! Human beings are the only ones who don't all look alike.) We were waiting, finally, for *The Hundred Headless Woman* because we knew that Max Ernst is the only one today to have harshly repressed in his own person any concern (in anyone who tries to express himself) with less interesting "forms"; in this regard, any complacency leads one to intone the idiotic hymn of the "three apples," as Cézanne and Renoir finally did, and all the more grotesquely for putting on airs. Because we knew that Max Ernst was not the kind to shrink from anything that might widen the field of modern vision and provoke the innumerable *illusions of true recognition* that it is up to us, and us alone, to have in the future and the past. Because we knew that Max Ernst is the most magnificently haunted brain alive today, I mean the one who is least likely to let some tiny worry stand in his way, the one who knows it isn't enough to send another boat out into its worldly course, even if it's a pirate ship, but that you have to rebuild the *arc* – and in such a way that this time, it won't be the dove returning, but the crow.

The Hundred Headless Woman will be the supreme picture book for the present age, in which it will become increasingly clear that each sitting room has sunk "to the bottom of a lake," and this means (let there be no mistaking it) with all its fish candelabra, its stellar gilding, its dancing grasses, its muddy depths, and its garb of reflections. Such is our idea of progress, on the eve of the year 1930, that we are for once happy and impatient to see the eyes of children, wide with future promise, open like butterflies at the edge of this lake while, for their wonder and our own, the black lace mask falls from the first hundred faces of the fairy.

1929

The First Dalí Exhibit

"Sterilize."

— DALÍ

ALÍ APPEARS HERE AS A MAN who might hesitate (and whom the future will show did not hesitate) between talent and genius, as once we would have said between vice and virtue. He is the kind of person who comes from far enough away so that when you see him entering, and only entering, you don't have time to see him at all. Without saying a word, he places himself in a system of interferences.

On the one hand, there are the moths that claim to get into his clothes and not to leave him even when he goes out in the streets. These moths say good things about Spain and even Catalonia; that it is just glorious that a man should paint such little things so well (and even better when he paints *large*), that a person with a shit-stained shirt, like the one in *The Lugubrious Game*, is worth ten men fully dressed and, still more so, a hundred naked men; and that it is high time that vermin should rule the streets in our dear country and its wasted capital. Finally, now that Surrealism is dead, the professional mourners, whose triumphant "documentation" we are supposed to be (having been kicked in the teeth), and now that the cops have regained their prerogatives as at very least *honorable folks* – after all, you aren't hoping to change the world, are you? – we might be able to assimilate quietly lots of tough things (so say the moths, after which they spread out in all the old fashion magazines, in whatever remains of abstract painting – ? – in criticism where they claim to make a "revolution of the word," in the politics of the anti-Communist left, and in the truly delicious and really sugary stuff of talking movies).

On the other hand, there is hope: the hope that everything will not crumble after all, that the admirable voice that is Dalí's will not break in his own ear (for starters), since certain "materialists" want to confuse this voice with the squeaking of his own polished shoes. We believe we are winning the case we have brought against reality, and that is why, as of right now, we mean to produce, giving it a particular aura, the pathetic witness of a man who, more than any other, seems to us to have nothing to save – *nothing, not even his head*. So long as we live, no matter what, they will not plant the ignoble flag of country, art, or discomfiture in the Cimmeria, the only new place we have discovered lately and that we mean to keep for ourselves. Dalí, who reigns over these distant countrysides, must know of too numerous and too shameful examples to let himself be stripped of his marvelous land of treasures. May it please the powers whose envoy he is in the world and among us that he forever keep his eyes closed to the miserable plans for *bridges* that greed and spite will conspire to make him cast across the sparkling, unapproachable, and magnetic river... Perhaps, with Dalí, this is the first time that the mental windows can open wide and that we can feel ourselves gliding toward an opening into the savage sky. We are literally seized (and that isn't the least of it) by the sight of that lion's head, huge as anger, or of that mask with its handle that I don't yet want to think about – for I am afraid – and that seem to want to turn infinitely, their expressions unchanging, not only in these paintings but within us, yes, in a sort of interior window, glancing off each other *in the air* as if the latter were suddenly to reveal itself as a simple play of mirrors that we need only modify, imperceptibly but surely, to bring forth an immense gap in which those figures (imaginary or not), would finally appear who haunt a second landscape, a second zone that everything lets us foresee. What could those strange scarabs possibly want, as they roll that enormous ball in front of them, behind them, stumbling but never weary, as we seem to be trying to roll the earth? Life is given to humans with seductions rather like the ones that the language of the anteater must offer ants.

No question about it, we still have to shake off both what oppresses us on the moral level and what "physically," as they say, keeps us from seeing clearly. If only, for example, we didn't have those famous trees! And those houses, and volcanoes, and empires... The secret of Surrealism lies in the fact that we are convinced that something is hiding behind them. Yet we need only to examine the possible methods of suppressing those trees to see that only one of those methods remains to us, that in the long run everything depends on our power of *voluntary hallucination*. When you think about it, the focus of our attention should be the place where all our most suspect feelings come to light. We can expect a great deal from a methodical assault of these feelings against life.

Dalí's art, the most hallucinatory we know so far, constitutes a real threat. Totally new beings with obvious bad intentions have just started out. It's a dark joy to see how nothing happens on their path except themselves and to recognize, in their way of multiplying and *melting*, that they are beasts of prey.

November 1929

*Lyubovnaya lodka razbilas o byt**

MAYAKOVSKY'S SUICIDE, which occurred on April 14, 1930, highlights the problematic relations that could exist in the best of men between the assurances he gives (and in all good faith believes he can give) of his unconditional devotion to the *cause* that he deems most justified – in this case, the revolutionary cause – and the fate that life hands him as a specific individual: life that brushes aside anyone who does not have a taste for self-preservation pure and simple; life that wields the terrible weapon (among others) of the concrete versus the abstract. "Be a revolutionary if you like. With your feeble strength, you might even help transform the world. For all you'll know! [Followed by a grand panorama of the centuries.] On the other hand, this woman is so beautiful – look closely! She is perhaps the only one you will ever love, and who will ever love you. You'd like to know whether she shares, or better still whether you can make her share, your belief in a new order, or in one that is yet to come? Whether she will not cause you to doubt that very belief? She is beautiful, they say. And they even add, as a further distraction, that she is blonde or dark. At the rate we're going – careful, my friend, in any case you'll soon be dead – just a glimpse of her will make it impossible for you to act as if you didn't place this woman above *all else.*"

Please understand, it is not I who am speaking this way, but life that uses this curious language. Fragile images – let's not deny it, we aren't old enough – from a world that we have helped

* "Love's boat has smashed against the daily grind."

edify, a world that will be more tolerable when we are no longer here. There is nothing in it that cannot be resolved, at least momentarily, in the madness of a kiss – a kiss between a man and the woman he loves, and only that woman. In this domain, let others debate the legitimacy of an inexplicable yet categorical choice, about which the least we can say is that it is not based on purely intellectual seduction. It might simply be that the human race, despite or because of the scant consideration we give our own life, uses seduction in order to make us face up to its incomprehensible demands: you risk having a child. Such a speculation, insofar as (no doubt) everyone unconsciously indulges in it, is enough to render all thought suspect. Mayakovsky, while alive, was powerless against it, and so am I: certain breasts are just too lovely.

But what a constant tragedy if that indestructible ideal ("Tell Ermilov it's a shame he abandoned the watchword; the point was to win"), the ideal that, whenever we must envision possessing no more than ourselves – and even love, alas!, affords us many such opportunities – makes us tend to see the successive conditions of our life, joy, pain, as miserable accidents: what a tragedy if that ideal should find in the non-reciprocity of love (even if only apparent), or in the very feminine misunderstanding of how such an ideal can viably subsist without damaging love, a reason for its own retreat or collapse! A revolutionary can love a non-revolutionary, or even – although I'm less certain about this – a counter-revolutionary. It goes without saying that the situation of women in contemporary society leads the most physically favored among them to, at the very least, undervalue revolutionary action: we can understand their particular dread of any new selection criteria. I repeat that in addition – and will Socialism have any power to change this? – they have an inborn horror of anything that is not done strictly out of love for them. Will these unfortunate attitudes result in bona fide revolutionaries avoiding such women at all costs, and taking refuge, when they need love, far away from them, in a world of triviality and disgrace?

To love or not to love, that is the question – the question that a revolutionary should be able to answer without a second thought. And let it be understood that we have no time for the grotesque responses that such a declaration cannot fail to elicit from human garbage of every stripe. Nothing would indicate, and I'll say no more than this, that the man who has reached the highest degree of social conscience (namely, the revolutionary) enjoys any greater protection against the danger of a woman's gaze: that gaze which, if it turns away, plunges the mind into darkness; but which, even if it does not turn away, still cannot shed light. After all, that man never said he wanted to stop being seen as a man. Does the need you might have of another person's presence, to the exclusion of everyone else, constitute a flaw, on which those who do not feel this need have a right – again, from the revolutionary standpoint – to judge you?

We persist here in trying to deduce one's revolutionary duty from one's general duties as a human being, from human duty as we are able to conceive of it in the place we occupy. And it would be pointless trickery to pretend we could act otherwise. Trotsky writes a bit cursorily (though, it's true, for a highly informed group of readers): "Mayakovsky came to the revolution via the shortest road, that of rebellious bohemia." Bohemia? I'd like to know what he means by that. I believe that poetry itself is at stake. A real distaste for happiness, at least of any duration; a fundamental inability to make peace with life, the stupidity and pettiness of which man can never remedy to any significant degree – I don't mean to belittle the moral importance of social action, the only effective kind; but what can one do against mud (in the physical sense), against external and internal dissipation, against wear and tear, against slowness, against sickness? – a certain indifference toward the future, fatal for those who are irrevocably condemned to pay in emotions that are much too dear: if these must be deemed the poet's distinctive traits, I find it hard to believe that it's with words such as "bohemia," or with conventional allusions to literary cafés or pipe smoke (?), that they can accuse Mayakovsky (or, on a different scale, Rimbaud) of conservative individualism. I am elaborating on this necessarily partial appreciation, made as it was by a political revolutionary about a revolutionary poet, only because it threatens to blind a few well-meaning souls who feel that Mayakovsky, because of certain responsibilities he had assumed, did not have the right to put an end to his life. (Are we in the world, yes or no? In other words, have we been put here by persons who basically intended for us to be or not be in it and, if only by reason of this fact, can't we be the judge of whether to stay or leave? We might even be granted the most unimpeachable freedom. But if we do not feel in complete control of our fate, then what transcendent law should paralyze the idea, in us, of the social disappearance of our vague and ill-defined "cell"?) Pipe smoke... indeed, it's through the smoke of a thousand pipes, to which we take the liberty of adding the smoke of a thousand or more factory chimneys, that we might try to get a positive idea of our individual *necessity*. To act always presupposes some small amount of caprice that only (and by definition) true men of action are apt to misjudge, but that in the eyes of philosophers and poets retains all its epiphenomenal value: the epiphenomenon resides in just how long one can ponder a disturbing situation before being pushed into action – which is itself infinitely hopeful. Contrary to what "mainstream" man would have us believe (and proud as he is to carry on his broad shoulders his little termite's head), anything at all stirring in the world rests on a feeling of *after we're gone* that, in life itself, wastes no opportunity to grapple with the paltry *while we're at it*. After we walked down this street… meanwhile, in the next room… while our backs were turned… the twenty-first century. From this permanent duel with its uneven pleasures – this duel whose outcome, on open ground freshly and imperceptibly disturbed, is never in doubt – the marvelous beast with steady eyes and stabbed heart called courage is reborn at every moment. Courage, moreover, does not lie in the choice between staying alive or dying, but rather in gazing cold-bloodedly upon the respective violence of these two contradictory currents that carry us along. A thinking man, in other words an honest man, is called upon at every moment to make the final judgment and, figuratively or not, I consider it healthy that his hand does not let go of the pistol. The issue of whether he did or did not betray is not to be raised for Mayakovsky; for such men, the only question is whether their strength did or did not betray them. But Mayakovsky was still young, so should I plead illness in his case? Yes, if we mean the splendid, incurable illness that love is for certain beings: "Where is that woman? I want to see her." "It's over, we tell you." "She's dead!" "Not at all. She's in the arms of a cretin, and at this very moment she is laughing. Oh! she's no longer thinking of you… Who is he? An embassy attaché, a bourgeois – unless, hang on a moment, unless he's a revolutionary the likes of which you've never seen: he gets most of his income from manufacturing beds… you know, for Clairvaux prison."* "Yes, I

* For example. [The double allusion in this passage suggests how Breton has superimposed his own unhappy affair with Suzanne Muzard onto Mayakovsky's love for Tatiana Iakovleva: the "bourgeois attaché" refers to Iakovleva's

know. She despised him. But what about her, just tell me about her; the man is unimportant. Is she happy? what does she dream about? how is she wearing her hair?"

Philosophers approach the world in their own way, and that's no small statement if we consider the abyss of incomprehension that separates them, and will long continue to separate them, from common mortals. They manage to confront the harsh light of criticism – once again, the kind that, at a certain point, pushes men to act and turns a page of history – only through a large number of intermediaries who have no qualms (and rightly so) about using for increasingly practical ends what was initially no more than the inner illumination of a single mind; or if need be about performing, with their eyes fixed on the last row of the gallery, the most indispensable sleight of hand: from Hegel to the present day. I put it above doubt that the dialectical materialism of Marx and Engels, insofar as, by all appearances, it is resolved and can only be resolved in a revolutionary imperative, finds itself before a concrete task of such urgency that those who are imbued with the greatness, not to say the difficulty, of this task are authorized to gloss over various minor objections that one might make from the philosophical viewpoint. For instance, I'm not entirely sure how solid Engels's charges against Feuerbach really are,* at least as concerns the return to idealism via the apologia of sexual love: "And so sexual love and the intercourse between the sexes is apotheosized [by Feuerbach] to a *religion,* merely in order that the word religion, which is so dear to idealistic memories, may not

impending marriage to a viscount, said to be one of the contributing factors to the poet's suicide; while "beds for Clairvaux prison" aims directly at Breton's rival (and Suzanne's new husband), Emmanuel Berl, whose father managed such a factory in the town of Clairvaux.—*trans.*]

* Cf. Engels, *Ludwig Feuerbach and the End of Classical German Philosophy.*

disappear from the language." I'm afraid that the end of that sentence is not very serious; or rather I fear that Engels, who accustomed us to greater severity, is indulging in nothing more than a little fist-pounding. The downfall of the idea of religion, as Feuerbach was perhaps the first to advocate it, justly devoting all his energies toward that end, remains in our eyes an admirable work whose teachings we will still want to study even after the global Revolution.

With what regret does Engels go on to say: "Sexual love in particular has undergone a development and won a place during the last 800 years which has made it a compulsory pivotal point of all poetry during this period." (This statement, moreover, has now lost much of its rigor, as Rimbaud and especially Lautréamont have since then prodigiously expanded the problematic of poetry by setting entirely different limits to the communicability and expression of human emotions.) It is nonetheless the case, if we take a moment to observe the perceptible world, that the love of a man for a woman, beyond the immemorial and senile slobberings to which it has given rise in literature, persists in clogging the air with huge flowers and wild beasts. For the mind, which always needs to feel it is in a safe place, it remains the most terrible of stumbling blocks. Poets approach the world in their own way, and that's no small statement if we consider... (see above). Upon them still weighs, we have to admit, in 1930, the threat that the world can be made barren by the loss of a single person, as one poor wight said in a verse that deserved infinitely better than to have been written by him. Just as philosophers are liable to rock to sleep, on a counterfeit ocean, the capricious spirit of human *accomplishment* that alternately enjoys and chafes at effort – and this regardless of the true wind that, after their deaths, will bring to the protuberances of their skulls all the respect due the bumps on a nutshell – so poets still are and perhaps always will be subject to the illusion (more tragic in human terms) by which the irreparable loss of the one they love cannot fail, by urging them toward death, to shatter the mirror of the world before their very eyes. Will we reach the point, in the interests of public health, of denying them the right to choose in matters of love: a right that is so vital to them and that they have nonetheless so frequently misused against themselves (and consequently against more than themselves)? In all probability the poetic vocation, just like the philosophic vocation, and whether the sociologists like it or not, cannot be denied.

This apparent derision: a person's inability, revolutionary though he might be, to place the loftiest common good above the personal ill that such an adventure can entail – so much so that he no longer finds a way to keep on living, if only *to see what happens* – is still not a valid cause for skepticism, in revolutionary terms. Personally, I'm more beholden to Mayakovsky for having put the "immense talent" that Trotsky recognized in the service of the successful Russian Revolution than for having, on his own behalf, compelled public admiration with the dazzling imagery of "Cloud in Trousers." I love sight unseen, that is to say *in complete confidence,* those propaganda posters and proclamations he drafted, with all the talent he could muster, to celebrate the triumph of the first proletarian republic. Nothing will prevent me from considering them the "summits of his creation." It is at the very least unexpected, not to say distressing, to hear some revolutionaries complain that they didn't contain enough lyricism. Lyricism... But under such circumstances, aren't a certain reserve and austerity the height of luxury? They are what help me understand Mayakovsky's very simple disappearance under other circumstances, since one can just as well speak of other circumstances with regard to poets: "Comrade Government"... "Life and I are even"... "the taxes." – Honesty.

And now a few words about the riffraff. A certain Habaru, in *Le Soir* and *Monde,* has tried to exploit Mayakovsky's suicide at our expense, and in general at the expense of all those who, with Mayakovsky, proclaim the absolute inanity of supposedly proletarian literature:

> We cannot judge Mayakovsky's poetry without recalling his Futurist origins. Before the war, the Futurist movement had reached its most violent expression in economically backward countries such as Italy and Russia. Futurism was essentially imperialistic, and tried to create art that would express the dynamism of the imperialist era. What inspired it was movement rather than the forms that determine movement or the objectives they rush toward. This purely individualistic inspiration led Marinetti to glorify war and fascism. *By the same token,** it led Mayakovsky to glorify the proletarian revolution.

Such impudent allegations are not even worth protesting. Once again, someone is trying to pass off the expressive technique for the thing expressed. Of course Futurism, as an enterprise seeking to renew artistic forms and reacting against academic decadence, won around 1913 the adherence of writers and artists from Germany, America, and France, as well as Italy and Russia. If Futurist art sought to express "the dynamism of the imperialist era," how could Mayakovsky, as a Futurist, have been so opposed to the war from the moment it broke out? How could he, in 1915, have called for and predicted the Russian Revolution? The whole

* My emphasis.

thing wouldn't be worth a shrug if this miserable line of argument hadn't managed to crop up again in *L'Humanité* – that is, in the only place in France where Mayakovsky might have expected to be defended, at very least. In an article signed G. G., filled with the most nauseating platitudes (and finally disavowed in a second, anonymous article), Mayakovsky is again portrayed as a bourgeois ill-adapted to ideas of proletarian emancipation, who revealed himself as such by his self-inflicted death. "His words are not devoted to the life of labor and pain lived by the exploited and enslaved proletariat, as are, for example, those of Damian Biedny, from the Tsarist epoch before 1917... Nor is he the bard of that robust and vigorous effort that characterizes the working class, bursting with strength and joy, full of revolutionary fervor and irresistible in its final triumph...," etc.

Now that Mayakovsky is dead, we refuse more than ever to sanction this undermining of the spiritual and moral stance he had taken. We deny, for a long time to come, any possible existence to poetry or art that would adopt the extreme simplification – *à la* Barbusse – of ways of thinking and feeling. We are still waiting for someone to show us a "proletarian" work of art. The exhilarating life of the struggling proletarian; the staggering, ruinous life of a mind delivered to its own beasts: as far as we're concerned, it would be pointless not to try to combine these two separate dramas into one. On this score, let no one expect any concessions from us.

July 1930

On the Relations between
Intellectual Labor and Capital

What are your thoughts on the current role of capital vis-à-vis intellectual producers?

Are those who exploit literary and artistic production fulfilling their duties toward the arts and letters?

With respect to bookstores, theaters, musical works, the cinema, the daily and periodical press, and the sale of works of art, do you have any optimistic or pessimistic observations to make concerning the relations between intellectual Labor and those who bring it to fruition?

Do you believe that these relations require any modifications or improvements? Please specify.

Do you feel that artistic producers would be well advised to create associations to help them exploit their work themselves? If so, how would you envision such associations? (L'Esprit français, August 15, 1930)

To avoid any confusion from the outset, we must distinguish between two principal modes of "intellectual" production: first, the kind that aims at satisfying man's *spiritual appetite*, which is as natural as physical hunger; and second, the kind that aims at satisfying the producer's needs of an entirely different order (money, honors, fame, etc.). The age-old coexistence of these two tendencies, combined with the second's efforts to appear identical to the first, is liable to smother the true debate, which you might not wish to launch.

Indeed, it hardly matters whether the services rendered by capital to that second class of producers — in jobs, tips, or crosses

– rewards them more or less than equitably for their zeal in ideologically promoting this capital, by taking up the daily defense of its army, its church, its police, its laws, and its mores. Such an individual is an integral part of the capitalist world and the extent of his setbacks in that world will never morally exceed that of any other exploiter – let's say, to be colorful, a rubber merchant.

The intellectual producer I wish to consider, leaving the other kind aside, is the one who, through his products, mainly tries to satisfy the needs of his own mind. "A thing can be useful," says Marx, "and the product of human labor, without being a commodity. Whoever directly satisfies his wants with the produce of his own labor, creates, indeed, use-values, but not commodities. In order to produce the latter, he must not only produce use-values, but use-values for others, social use-values." Let us note that the problem, considered from an intellectual perspective, is complicated by the fact that these social use-values might take a very long time to mature: Baudelaire wracked with debts, his heirs growing richer and richer. We can deduce from this, on the one hand, that Baudelaire was frustrated in his need for the material security to which he had a right in exchange for his labor (and this by virtue of every law of economic equivalency); on the other hand, since Baudelaire's case can represent the entire category of genuine searchers in question here, that in a capitalist regime the same conditions apply both to certain very rare productions of the mind and to the extraction of precious minerals – such as diamonds, and still according to Marx – which the actual miners never get "paid for at their full value."

The professional regulation of intellectual labor thus conceived is and always will be impossible in bourgeois society: first, because such regulation can be justified only by a qualitative judgment that historically has proven to be not that of the artist's contemporaries but (nearly always in contradiction to contemporary judgments) that of posterity; and second, because it is impossible to appraise its value by the common measure of workhours. (If a poet spends a day writing a poem, and the cobbler the same amount of time making a pair of shoes, the fact remains that these two objects are not interchangeable, and that while the cobbler can always start up again the following day, the poet can't necessarily do the same.)

I hasten to add that, naturally, in this domain I am against any immediate demand, and that I mean to limit myself here to demonstrating the absolute antagonism that exists between the conditions for independent thought, which ultimately – though too late for the thinker – wins out over human cowardice, and the conditions for temporary equilibrium in a world where it is far more effective in every respect to consider that on the average "for every hour of labor, capitalism claims half... without pay." Until that crushing debt is paid in full, it behooves us not to wipe away the specifically intellectual grievances which, to the extent that they are well-founded, should not take the form of vain corporate undertakings, but rather must convince those who are suffering from the current order of things to serve without reservations, and as if it were their own, the admirable cause of the proletariat.

October 1930

Psychiatry Standing before Surrealism

> But I will rise up in protest, I will call infamy down
> upon the head of the witness for the prosecution, I
> will cover him with shame! Can you imagine being
> a witness for the prosecution?... How horrible!
> Only humanity could come up with such monstrosi-
> ties! Is any barbarity more refined, more civilized
> than the witness for the prosecution?...
>
> In Paris, there are two dens, one for thieves, the
> other for murderers. The den of thieves is the Stock
> Exchange; the den of murderers is the Palace of
> Justice.
>
> — PÉTRUS BOREL

TO MY KNOWLEDGE, ten newspapers — *Les Nouvelles littéraires, L'Oeuvre, Paris-Midi, Le Soir, Le Canard enchaîné, Le Progrès médical, Vossische Zeitung, Le Rouge et le Noir, La Gazette de Bruxelles,* and *Le Moniteur du Puy-de-Dôme* — have reported on the controversy raised by the Société Médico-Psychologique over a passage in my book *Nadja*: "I know that if I were mad, after several days of confinement I should take advantage of any *lapses* in my madness to murder anyone, prefer-ably a doctor, who came near me. At least this would permit me, like the violent, to be confined in solitary. Perhaps they'd leave me alone." Most of these newspapers, moreover, being mainly preoc-cupied with casting the incident in a humorous light, limited them-selves to commenting on the ridiculous response of Pierre Janet: "The works by the Surrealists are above all confessions of men obsessed, and men who doubt," and to hauling out the usual jokes that always seem in season any time a psychiatrist complains about a patient, a colonist about a colonized, a policeman about the person he is arresting (arbitrarily or not). But no one has bothered to refute the staggering claims of Dr. de Clérambault – who, not content with taking the opportunity to demand that the "authorities" protect him from the Surrealists, people who according to him dream only of "saving themselves the trouble of thinking" (*sic*), went on to maintain that psychiatrists should be safeguarded against the risk of forced retirement... should one of them decide to kill an escaped or freed patient by whom he felt threatened. In such cases, it seems, a solid pecuniary compensation would suffice.* It is clear that psychiatrists, used to treating the mentally ill like dogs, are amazed at not being allowed, even outside their practice, to put them down.

Given these declarations, we might imagine that Mr. de Clérambault could find no better outlet for his brilliant faculties than in the prison system, and indeed he wears the title of head doctor at the special infirmary of the jail nearest the Prefecture of Police. It would be surprising if a consciousness of that caliber, a mind of that quality hadn't found the means to put itself entirely at the disposal of the bourgeois police and justice system. May I say, however, that some of us consider this compromise sufficient grounds for denying (with no insult intended to science) the epithet *learnèd* to men who, like the scandalous Mr. Amy in the Almazian affair, primarily serve the instruments of social repression? Yes, I say here that one must have lost all sense of human dignity (or indignity) to dare appear in court in the role of *expert witness.* Who can forget the edifying disputes between psychiatric experts at the trial of the criminal mother-in-law, Mme. Lefèvre,

* Cf. *Annales médico-psychologiques* (November 1929).

in Lille? During the war, I saw just how much importance the military courts accorded medico-legal reports – or rather, that the psychiatric experts let them accord those reports, since they continued to give their opinions while the harsh penalties sometimes went so far as to condemn their rare requests for acquittal, based on a recognition of the defendant's "total" irresponsibility. How can we believe that the civilian courts are more enlightened, that the experts are in a better moral position, when: first, Article 64 of the Penal Code allows for acquitting the accused only in cases where all agree that he "was in a state of dementia at the time of the action, or that he was obliged to commit this action by a force he could not resist" (which is philosophically incomprehensible); second, scientific "objectivity," which in this domain claims to be an auxiliary to the illusory "impartiality" of justice, is in itself a utopian notion; third, it is well understood – since in reality society means to punish not the guilty man, but the antisocial one – that the issue is first and foremost to slake public opinion, that vile beast incapable of accepting that infractions should not be suppressed because the individuals who committed them were ill only during those infractions, such that medical sequestration, accepted as a punishment if need be, no longer has any justification?*

I say that the doctor who agrees, under such conditions, to speak before a tribunal, unless it is systematically to maintain the complete irresponsibility of the accused, is a cretin or a swine, which comes down to the same thing.

If we take into account, moreover, the recent evolution of psychiatry, and this strictly from a psychological viewpoint, we will note that its main procedure increasingly consists in the abu-

* Whence the gratuitous, jesuitical, nauseating notion of "mitigated responsibility."

sive denunciation of what, after Bleuler, has been called *autism* (egocentricity), a very convenient denunciation that allows the bourgeois to deem "pathological" anything in man that is not a pure and simple adaptation to the external conditions of life, since it secretly aims to eliminate every case of refusal, insubordination, or desertion that until now might or might not have seemed worthy of respect (poetry, art, passionate love, revolutionary action, etc.). Autistic today: the Surrealists (for Mr. Janet — and no doubt Mr. Claude). Autistic yesterday: a young physics teacher examined at the Val-de-Grâce because, drafted into the nth air force regiment, he "lost no time in displaying his lack of interest in the army and told his comrades about his horror of the war, which in his view was just organized murder." (In the words of Dr. Fribourg-Blanc, who has published the results of his observations in the February 1930 issue of the *Annales de médecine légale*, this subject showed "evident schizoid tendencies." You be the judge: "Pursuit of isolation, internalization, lack of interest in any practical endeavor, morbid individualism, idealistic conceptions of universal brotherhood.") Autistic tomorrow: by the infamous testimony of these gentlemen, in other words removable at any moment from the path on which their conscience alone has put them, in other words *confiscable at will,* all those who persist in not acclaiming the watchwords behind which this society hides in an attempt to make each of us, without exception, participate in its misdeeds.

We hereby claim the honor of being the first to sound the alarm and to rise up against the unacceptable and increasing abuse of power by people whom we are inclined to see less as doctors than as jailers, and especially as suppliers for prisons and scaffolds. *Because they are doctors,* we forgive them least of all for having indirectly assumed these sordid executioner's chores.

However Surrealist or "methodist" we might be in their eyes, we cannot urge them too strongly, even if some of them should accidentally fall under the blows of those they are arbitrarily seeking to diminish, to have the decency to keep their mouths shut.

1930

Letter to André Rolland de Renéville

DEAR SIR: Your article "The Most Recent State of Surrealist Poetry," published in the February issue of *La Nouvelle Revue française,* is not the kind to leave one indifferent to its author's objections. If you will permit me, I will try to answer some of them.

1. You say it was wrong of me, in the *Second Manifesto of Surrealism,* to try to topple some of the poetic idols who still stood – Baudelaire, Rimbaud, Poe – and to let myself get carried away by an increasingly negativistic delirium of purity that pushed me to make some rather perfunctory judgments.

Since you yourself state, after examining Surrealism's evolution over the past few years, that the Surrealists' literary activity can no longer be meaningfully isolated from their political activity, don't you think that the necessary reconciliation of these two would force us to react violently against anything that, in the final account, might absurdly speak of expiation, shamefully preach resignation, or scandalously militate in favor of conservatism? From a revolutionary standpoint, I can't help it if certain works of great "literary" merit have begun to crack apart. I persist in believing that the fate of those works does not lie strictly in themselves, and I maintain that any criticism worthy of the name should hold them responsible for their byproducts and outgrowths. An outgrowth of Poe's works? Look at the January 23 issue of *Le Journal,* in which a cop writes to Clément Vautel: "As for the vocation of policeman, nine times out of ten it is inspired by reading the stories of Poe, Conan Doyle, Gaboriau, etc." It is true, says this individual, that "a young man who adopted the methods of Mr. Dupin" wouldn't necessarily be guaranteed "practical success," but the rest is only a matter of training and patience. You will agree that any mentor chosen by the modern police force cannot be one of ours.

2. The current of general disaffection to which you feel we have bowed suggests to you that Eluard and I, in the central part of our book *The Immaculate Conception*, allowed ourselves to show signs of mistrust toward automatic writing and other forms of "non-directed" mental expression. Supposedly, therefore, we are gradually renouncing the Surrealist method itself, and already the first step has been taken on the path back to what Tzara, in the fourth issue of *Le Surréalisme ASDLR*, calls "poetry as a means of expression." I can assure you that it is nothing of the sort. First of all, we have never claimed any Surrealist text whatsoever as a *perfect* example of verbal automatism. Even in the most "non-directed" text, we must admit, one can notice a certain friction – though I haven't despaired of eliminating it completely, by a means yet to be discovered. It is nonetheless the case that a minimum of direction subsists, usually in the guise of an *arrangement into poetry*. It is hard to avoid the more or less utilitarian reasons for doing it this way. Given this, what could be more tempting than to replace this particular determination of ours with a different one, whatever it might be, and however specific, so long as words are not made to turn around and around *for nothing*? It seemed to us, for example, that this determination could well be the cluster of symptoms currently defined as pathognomic of a given mental illness. Thus conditioned, the word (unknown or not) that we were awaiting would surely break loose in a way that is, on many levels, more gripping than it might otherwise be. Indeed, we knew that thought possesses only a limited number of *alarm signals* to manifest its extreme disturbances. What would

happen if these signals were willfully maneuvered, in more or less autonomous groupings, corresponding to means of linkage unearthed by psychiatric analysis? Not only would we do away with the poetic obsession, the principal cause of error, but we would also gain by pitting against language a mode of thought hypothetically stricken in several of its most vulnerable points. As we might have predicted, psychic automatism filled the boundaries we had set for it with extraordinary force. It seems impossible to speak of *directed* thought under such conditions. Rather, one could say that we wagered on what we knew to be this thought's chosen means of losing itself, by removing any obligation of immediate exchange between human beings. Apart from the "Attempted Simulation of Interpretative Delirium" – a delirium involving the hypertrophy of the reasoning faculties, which alone kept us from reproducing it convincingly – we believe we have, without pastiche, easily managed to convey clinically acceptable monologues. As for experiencing the corresponding states of consciousness along the way, that was never our claim. The main interest of the experiment lay in the fact that, from the texts we obtained, we could probably have provided original insights into the mechanism of certain graphic alterations contained in them – which psychiatry, still hypnotized by the manifest content of patients' ravings, has so far done no more than catalog. I hope that Surrealism, surmounting any concern for the picturesque, will soon move on to interpreting the automatic texts – poetic or otherwise – that it labels with its name; as far as I can see, the apparent oddity of these writings will not stand the test. We have good reason to think that this systematic undertaking will end up reducing considerably the supposedly irreducible field of anomalies in certain languages. It is worth noting that J. Lévy-Valensi, Pierre Migault, and Jacques Lacan, authors of an article on a case of schizography published in the December 1931 issue of the *Annales médico-psychologiques,* rightly insist on the "remarkable poetic value" of certain passages in their patient's letters. It's a sign of the times that poetry, even in the eyes of the medical profession, has shattered the barriers behind which people strove so ingeniously to cloister it. Allow me to draw your attention to this statement by the above-mentioned authors: "The experiments conducted by certain writers on a kind of writing that they call 'Surrealist,' whose method they have described very scientifically, show the remarkable degree of economy that graphic automatism can attain without the use of hypnosis. In these productions, certain parameters, such as an overall rhythm or sentence structure, can be set in advance without diminishing the violently disparate nature of the resulting imagery." Judging from these statements, Eluard and I, by submitting to the written simulation of various forms of delirium, would not have overly compromised the Surrealist ambition of shedding some *authentic* light on the provisionally condemned areas of the human mind.

3. A paragraph in the *Second Manifesto,* where I deal with certain abrupt (and to me, suspect) changes in attitude, leads you to cast doubt on the qualifications of some of us Surrealists. I heartily deplore that in this regard your severity should be turned against René Char, author of pages that strike me as exceptionally *rare* in a wholly different sense from the one you mean. René Char will probably not forgive me for trying to justify his personal actions in *Méridiens,* a magazine that ceased publication in 1929 with a particularly lucid declaration by him, which matches on every point what his book *Arsenal* had led us to expect. I believe that the crystallization (in the Hegelian sense of "the moment at which the mobile and restless activity of magnetism

reaches complete repose") that Char constantly obtains from his thought lends every line of *Artine* or *L'Action de la justice est éteinte* an extreme transparency and hardness that are all his own, and that preserve him in particular from the Surrealist cliché – about which you and I agree, and which the magazine *Commerce* clearly welcomes. This hardness and transparency, for me, pass through Char's entire life, and necessarily mark both his poetry and his revolutionary convictions with the same sign. Moreover, these qualities are precisely the ones that Eluard and I considered liable to seal a truly intimate poetic collaboration (*Ralentir travaux*), which we believed could be realized better with three people than with two, the constantly variable third element serving as junction and resolution, and acting on the other two as a *unifying* factor. (This detail seems to have eluded Camille Schuwer and Gabriel Audisio, authors of a piece entitled "Poem in Common" that appeared in 1931 in *La Revue nouvelle*, which contains several interesting theoretical insights but offers up works whose components are much less tightly interwoven.)

4. While it is true that your article – which overall demonstrates admiration for Surrealism as a movement and a knowledge of its historical situation – gives me pause on only a few specific points, I confess that I cannot entirely understand the sudden about-face expressed between the first and last lines of your postscript. The more I think about it, the less I feel the two new issues of *Le Surréalisme au service de la Révolution* should prove to anyone, particularly to you, that we have suddenly and unexpectedly abandoned one position for another – to wit, the idealistic position for dialectical materialism. Didn't you yourself begin by noting that the confusion Surrealism causes literature lovers derives from the fact that "once poets understood that the sensory world is but one side of reality, whose other side is constituted by the

mind, they set out to escape the mental terrain that public opinion granted them, and to act in a domain that was but the prolongation of their own?" So what contradiction do you find between this attitude and the will that you very rightly ascribe to us to "act upon facts from now on"? It is quite true that we passed through idealism, and of the most subjective kind, but I can't believe that you would hold that passing phase of our thinking against us. It was in the essence of that thinking – as I'm sure you will concede – to broadly reproduce the evolution of philosophical thought over the past few centuries, and I persist in not seeing how one could go from mechanistic materialism to dialectical materialism without encountering idealism. Just as I persist in not seeing how, in the period of capitalist, imperialist, and colonialist savagery that we are living through, one could stop at the point where that encounter takes place. Surrealism's *total* commitment to dialectical materialism is clearly presented as an accomplished fact in the *Second Manifesto,* and since that time nothing has come along to diminish either the meaning or the breadth of that commitment. For my part, I resolutely maintain the conception of thought that continues to "oscillate between the awareness of its inviolate autonomy and that of its utter dependence." As far as I'm concerned, it is this, and this alone, that answers for the quality of Surrealist actions, whether Maxime Alexandre's or my own. It is also owing to this that I can count, for the future liberation of human thought, both on the sovereignty that in this thought alone is still unrealized yet remains potential, and on the *easily influenced* destiny of facts.

February 1932

On the Proletarian Literature Contest
Sponsored by *L'Humanité**

. . . .

W**E KNOW WHAT DISPARITIES** of language and thought have arisen, these past few years, over such a basically simple notion as proletarian literature. To tell the truth, I persist in thinking that the words "proletarian literature" are somewhat misguided, but, not being able to interpret them strictly literally, I believe the best thing is to try to see what they *tend to honor as use-value*. We need only recall here how the question was handled in this passage from the Kharkov resolutions** ("Resolution on the International Revolutionary and Proletarian Movement in Literature"):

> Proletarian literature is opposed in its essence, in other words by the very ideology of the working class, as it is expressed by proletarian writers in artistic forms they have created, to all of the past and present literature of other classes. The entire experience of humanity, its evolution and its struggle, and above all the class practice of the proletariat as a guide for all workers in

---

* Portions of a lecture given under the auspices of the Association des Ecrivains et Artistes Révolutionnaires at the Salle du Grand-Orient.

** The Kharkov conference, which took place in November 1930, consolidated a number of hard-line Communist positions toward writing, notably that the only acceptable brand of literature was the strictly proletarian variety – even as it publicly condemned several of Breton's own positions in the *Second Manifesto*. The resolutions themselves were published in 1931. [*trans.*]

the struggle for Socialism, and not as an interpreter of narrow corporate interests, finds its artistic expression in the work of proletarian writers. This ultimately determines the creation of new forms, which are specific to proletarian literature. We see this literature discovering new forms, which are opposed to the bourgeois literary tradition and respond to their own social content, by surpassing old genres and creating new ones. The writer's task is to add up the historical experience of class struggles – not as one who ponders or passively observes the facts, but as a champion of the Revolution who realizes the meaning of earlier stages of the proletarian movement for the future of class warfare. The method used by proletarian literature is dialectical materialism.

Examining this declaration closely, it might seem that there was no reason for the discussion to be so heated. Is it because they expressly state that "proletarian literature *is opposed* in its essence to all of the past and present literature of other classes"? It seems to me that this would be taking the word *opposition* in a not very dialectical sense. On the other hand, didn't Lenin clearly state that workers will never manage to participate in the elaboration of an independent ideology unless we make efforts to raise their level of consciousness? "It is necessary," he says in *What Is to Be Done?* "that the workers do not confine themselves to the artificially restricted limits of *'literature for workers'* but that they learn to an increasing degree to master *general literature.* It would be even truer," he adds, "to say 'are not confined,' instead of 'do not confine themselves,' because the workers themselves wish to read and do read all that is written for the intelligentsia, and only a few (bad) intellectuals believe that it is enough 'for workers' to be told a few things about factory conditions and to have repeated to them over and over again what has long been known." Let us not forget, as Lenin also said, that proletarian culture "is not clutched out of thin air; it is not an invention of those who call themselves experts in proletarian culture. That is all nonsense. Proletarian culture must be the logical development of the store of knowledge mankind has accumulated under the yoke of capitalist, landowner, and bureaucratic society."* To me, this seems sufficient to situate on its true dialectical plane the opposition between proletarian literature and the bourgeois literature treated in the Kharkov resolutions. Let me again point out that they also say that the passage of humanity's entire experience, its evolution and struggle, into the works of proletarian writers *"ultimately* determines the creation of new forms, which are specific to proletarian literature."* I'm stressing the word *ultimately,* which confers upon the sentence all of its dialectical significance. Does this mean that current forms used by the works summarily called "proletarian," whether in the capitalist countries or in Soviet Russia, must be seen as the definitive, accomplished forms of proletarian literature? Only those who cannot conceive of forms dynamically would make that mistake – in other words, those who expect these forms to be based on such fixed, immutable genres as the sonnet, for instance, or the classical tragedy in five acts. On the contrary, these forms must surely constitute only temporary molds that we should not take as models to be imitated in and of themselves. In short, I believe that we must guard against two deviations, in other words either underestimating or overestimating the possibilities for proletarian literature to exist today (naturally, the same considerations apply to proletarian art). Can such literature find its complete expression under the economic and

* V. I. Lenin, *The Tasks of the Youth Leagues.* [*trans.*]

social conditions that currently obtain in the world (edification of Socialism in the USSR, multiplication of capitalist contradictions in other countries)? No, I don't believe so. And not only do I not believe so, but I don't regret it. I don't regret it because if it were possible to completely realize proletarian art or literature, particularly in a capitalist regime, it would spell one less reason for us to topple that regime. Can we nonetheless say that proletarian literature is appearing on the horizon and is beginning to take shape in the most striking works coming out of Soviet Russia or Germany today? That this literature is, even now, in the process of being realized? Yes, we must say so. To my mind, this is how we should nuance our opinion of proletarian literature, which, let's not forget, can be no more than a transitional stage between the literature of bourgeois society and that of a classless society.

Insofar as it already exists, we can easily see that proletarian literature is the product more of a milieu than of a given individual. In fact, it can emanate only from a mass proletarian consciousness: I mean that it depends on the overall degree of emancipation of the working class in a given country. This is why we should expect to see its most typical manifestations, first in the USSR, where the fusion of worker-writers and "fellow travelers" is precipitated by the truly communal conditions they live under; then in Germany, where the heightening of class antagonisms following the application of the Versailles Treaty has united a particularly important *block* of revolutionary proletarian writers. In France, on the contrary, the supposed capitalist stabilization has until recently ended up hobbling the development of any literature that could be qualified, even in anticipation, as proletarian. But when that vulgar illusion is shattered by an economic crisis, then an Association such as ours must try by every means possible to determine the current that will favor the birth of such a literature and ensure its viability. Let us remember that according to the Kharkov resolutions themselves, "France is the country of the great traditions of popular art expressing a revolutionary and warlike ideology. It was in France that the working class first conquered its place in art, if only by serving as its theme; we need merely cite the names of Daumier, Courbet, and Zola. And it was in France that the best revolutionary hymns, the 'Carmagnole' and the 'Internationale,' were composed." These are, indeed, sufficient historical premises for us to envision a forthcoming reversal of the situation.

In a moment, in my conclusion, I'll say which conditions governing the work we do seem necessary for this reversal to take place – that is, for the literature of this country to reestablish its links with its true revolutionary tradition, while benefiting from the current contributions of Soviet literature and revolutionary literature from other countries. First, however, I should try to dispel some misconceptions in the minds of too many comrades regarding general literature, the kind that interests us as revolutionary writers and readers, insofar as it informs our notion of proletarian literature on the one hand and, beyond this, the literature of the classless society. I believe you will easily see that I am not straying from the subject of our contest. Reading the submissions has revealed, in fact, that the vast majority of our correspondents, in their use of written language, betray a certain number of influences that say a lot about their general knowledge and the state of their readings. Although it is a poor comfort, we can rightly stress that the greatest influence in this regard is exerted by the daily newspaper, in the articles, human interest items, stories, and serials that they more or less echoed. It seems quite evident that many comrades, for lack of time or money, read nothing else; and if we think of how most press articles are written, it should come as no surprise that a constant reading of them produces, in those who have no means of counterbalancing it, a neutral style, entirely sacrificed to pure information, stuffed with clichés, and utterly devoid of the particular virtues that might emerge from more studied forms of expression. Apart from this preponderant influence, the other visible influence is essentially exerted at a distance, in the absence of any valid competition, by a very small number of books read toward the end of childhood and of "selected excerpts" learned in school. Suffice it to say that these readings, in France, are determined by a good bourgeois concern with stocking local libraries, where the demand continues above all for the writings of Dumas *père*, Zola, Georges Ohnet, Hugo, Paul Féval, and Tolstoy. As for school recitations, drummed into students' heads for generations, you know that they are all culled from miserable literary study guides, which even bourgeois intellectuals have repeatedly decried, so obvious is it that their compilation was guided not by any concern for literary value, but on the contrary with a view toward exalting and glorifying the bourgeois family, homeland, and religion. You are all familiar with those imbecilic texts, which go from the idiocies of La Fontaine to the whimperings of André Theuriet, via Barbier's "Iambs." Well, Comrades, whether we like it or not, we have to admit that these pathetic first texts, to which human memory has already devoted far too much time, have not left us entirely unscathed, have not failed to contaminate our expressive faculties if some antidote didn't follow in their wake. Our examination of the many submissions for the contest, and especially of far too many poetic entries, leaves us without the slightest doubt on the subject.

From this, we can measure the full extent of the bourgeoisie's systematic efforts to paralyze the intellectual development of the working classes, thereby ensuring its passivity. At the end of primary school, where he was inculcated with odious lessons in resignation and ordered, to his greater detriment, to respect the established regime, the man who is forced to slave away *for others* is carefully kept under daily control by way of the newspapers. As you see, it's both simple and despicable.

In my view, such conditions – which, I repeat, are the main factor governing the formation of the worker's language – make it imperative for our Association to guide those of our comrades who have never been taught what to read, or who have never had the chance to learn for themselves, by establishing for them a reading plan that – apart from their strictly political texts – will truly benefit them. This is an actual pedagogical task that should not deter us; it's the best means we have of helping them fill the systematic and intentional gaps in their primary lay education. Note that in this regard, teaching really means counter-teaching. It is vital that our comrades learn to distinguish what is truly remarkable in a given text, even if that text bears no immediate relation to the class struggle (moreover, it's clear that the relation is always present, once one knows how to analyze these texts). I believe that in this way they will be able to react against the error that leads them to look with too exclusive, and often too blind, a sympathy upon the works of writers who have merely taken the proletariat as their theme, or even who have used their situation purely for revolutionary lip service. This is a good moment to recall the terms that Engels used in a letter to Bernstein of August 17, 1884, regarding the writer Jules Vallès, who nonetheless was often labeled a *proletarian*:

> You must not heap such compliments on Vallès. He is a dilettante or, even worse, a miserable phrasemaker and a worthless

fellow *who, due to lack of talent, has gone to extremes with ten-dentious junk to show his convictions, but it is really in order to gain an audience.*

It was the same Engels, as our comrade Fréville informed us three days ago in *L'Humanité,* who in April 1888 wrote to another socialist writer, Margaret Harkness, about an author whose royalist convictions should normally have kept him at a far remove:

Balzac whom I consider a far greater master of realism than all the Zolas *passés, présents et à venir,* in *La Comédie humaine* gives us a most wonderfully realistic history of French "Society," especially of *"le monde parisien,"* describing, chronicle-fashion, almost year by year from 1816 to 1848 the progressive inroads of the rising bourgeoisie upon the society of nobles, that reconstituted itself after 1815 and that set up again, as far as it could, the standard of *la vieille politesse française.** He describes how the last remnants of this, to him, model society gradually succumbed before the intrusion of the vulgar moneyed upstart, or were corrupted by him; how the grande dame, whose conjugal infidelities were but a mode of asserting herself in perfect accordance with the way she had been disposed of in marriage, gave way to the bourgeoisie, who horned her husband for cash or cashmere; and around this central picture he groups a complete history of French Society from which, even in economic details (for instance the rearrangement of real and personal property after the Revolution) I have learned more than from all the pro-

* In his essay, Breton cites the phrase as *"la vieille politique française"* – old French politics – rather than Engels's "old French politeness." [*trans.*]

fessed historians, economists, and statisticians of the period together.

And it was again the same Engels, we are told, who, asked to speak about the social value of Ibsen – whom some persisted in considering a reactionary and petit bourgeois – did not hesitate to state that in his opinion, Ibsen, a bourgeois writer, had brought about true progress. In our time, he said, we have learned nothing in literature except from Ibsen and the great Russian novelists:

> Ibsen, as spokesman for the bourgeoisie (which at the time was the progressive element), has enormous historical importance, both in this country and outside of it. Notably, Ibsen shows Europe and the world the need for the social emancipation of women. As Marxists, we cannot ignore this, and we must establish a distinction between the progressive bourgeois thinking of an Ibsen and the fearful, reactionary thinking of the German bourgeoisie. Dialectics requires this of us.

Just as we consider it our duty, in the philosophical sub-section of our organization's literary division, to set as our first practical task the drafting of a *study guide to dialectical materialism* (to realize the profound necessity of such a work, we need only cite this aphorism by Lenin, from his remarks on Hegel in the *Philosophical Notebooks,* which are still unpublished in French: "It is impossible to understand completely Marx's *Capital,* and especially its fifth chapter,* without having thoroughly studied and understood the *whole* of Hegel's *Logic.* Consequently, half a cen-

* *Sic:* in the original quote, Lenin specifies the *first* chapter. [*trans.*]

tury later none of the Marxists understood Marx!"); just as, I say, our role is to help rectify this state of affairs, if only in very modest proportions, it seems to me that one of the tasks that the specifically literary branch of our Association should assume is the compilation of a *Marxist study guide to general literature,* which would situate clearly, excluding all others, the authors and works whose historical importance (under the very wide angle in which Engels urges us to consider it) now seems undeniable. Since such a guide would necessarily be rather cursory, I could easily see it being supplemented, for our more advanced comrades, by a series of Marxist courses on general literature at the Workers' University – which, for our comrades who wish to write, would be a very useful complement to the *courses in Marxist literature.* We could, for example, successively study the French materialists, the political literature of the French Revolution, the Romantic period, the principal schools of historians, realism, naturalism, French poetry of the nineteenth century that actually warrants the name, etc. Furthermore, we would have every reason to place at the head of these accounts a critique – and if possible a revision – of the only Marxist theses that we have on the question, in other words Plekhanov's. Our Russian comrades, introducing them in the third and fourth issues of *Littérature de la Révolution mondiale,* have already expressed serious reservations about these theses, given their author's political and philosophical opportunism; and I believe that serious reservations of a literary and artistic order are also called for. Still and all, these theses, almost all of whose examples were taken from French literature and art, would provide us with a unique opportunity to objectivize and define our position on them.

. . . .

February 1933

Introduction to
Achim von Arnim's Strange Tales

A SURVEY IN WHICH I PARTICIPATED along with a certain number of individuals, comparing the merits of the principal imaginative works of the past century (poetry aside) and their impact on the artistic creation of our time, resulted in giving pride of place to a story by Achim von Arnim, followed very closely by another, both of which are included in the present volume.* In the apparent absence of any recent event that might account for this elective interest – the survey in question having been conducted without any prior exchange of opinions, and with each participant making his statement in total ignorance of the others' views – I believe that the resulting judgment stands as an objective value. The scope of this judgment is all the greater, its significance all the more worthy of being highlighted and defined, in that it tends (certainly not by chance in 1933) to elevate above a quantity of works that have always been held in high esteem a book that, at least in French translation, seems to have suffered particularly unjustly from inattention and neglect. The same, in fact, could be said of its author, whose name is never mentioned in France, and to whom even German literary history – entirely preoccupied with exalting the personality of his wife – rarely devotes much space. A few biographers, to be sure, have taken pains to deny responsibility for this state of affairs,

---

* This 1933 edition of Arnim's *Strange Tales* is a reprint of the 1856 translation by Théophile Gautier *fils*, newly prefaced by Breton and illustrated by Valentine Hugo. It contains three novellas: "Isabella of Egypt," "Maria Melück-Blainville," and "The Heirs to the Estate." [*trans.*]

attributing their neglect of Arnim to the persistent bad luck that has supposedly dogged him. To support their case, they cite the absence of chronological indications about his work – pointing out that the very date of his birth (January 26 or June 26) is contested – as well as the incompletion of his two novels *The Revelations of Ariel* and *Guardians of the Crown,* which to them seems related to the fact that since his death (although it has been attempted several times) no one has managed to bring out a complete edition of his works. Under this shadow of malediction Arnim's fearsome charm might well continue to operate all the more. Nonetheless, the time has come for anyone concerned with today's spiritual developments to meditate deeply on his talents and secrets.

To be concerned with these developments, even to penetrate their meaning to some small degree, does not imply that one can explain, from one century to the next, the return of certain ways of feeling that, in the past, have sometimes resorted to abstract and clearly divergent justifications. Apart from the wind of poverty that blows over it as it blew during most of Arnim's youth, Europe today would barely recognize itself in its image from back then. The illusions that pitted Schelling against Fichte, in the names of naturalistic mysticism and revolutionary criticism, have long come and gone. The increasing imbalance of States with their bitter economic rivalries, suspended in mutual distrust between two blood baths by the expedient settlements of treaties, gnawed from within by the ever more flagrant opposition of classes – all of this increasingly militates in favor of subordinating a theory of knowledge to a theory of action, of substituting a social ideal for the ideal of inner perfection. Still, we have to admit that there is something infinitely captivating about the latter, just as it was at the beginning of the nineteenth century, when it sought itself out in the brilliant enterprise of elucidation that consisted in the search for *Characteristics of the Present Age** and in the debate inspired by this publication. Otherwise, how could we explain that a literary testimony such as the one I've been asked to introduce here should resonate so marvelously in us? Sheltered from the degradation that a century has inflicted on the poor genius of men, there remains, as I have no hesitation in stating, the greatness – and therefore the task of explaining that greatness – of a man such as Arnim.

Everything keeps me from trying to persuade the reader of my enthusiasm at discovering the ever more original and incomparable beauties hidden in these three novellas, which were rather arbitrarily collected by Gautier under the superficial title *Strange Tales*. Poetic production, from Baudelaire to the present, has moreover tended to prepare the audience (which can only grow) for the intelligence and emotional achievement of these texts. Nor will I make the error of plunging, following some protagonist of Arnim's, into a maze of peregrinations from which a certain number of *literal* critics, even though they soon thought better of it, seem to have returned somewhat the worse for wear. If we look at his life, Arnim the man (despite his self-effacing manner) can give us greater insight into his deepest thoughts than Arnim the writer can. Arnim's faculty for transposition, however exceptional his talent might seem in this regard, must not conceal the things that gave rise to this transposition. It is there, at its very origin, that we must focus our investigation. When studying a work as richly inventive and vastly significant as Arnim's, we must ask ourselves what this work reflects; we must try to know whether, on closer inspec-

---

* Fichte.

tion, it isn't the product of an eminently favorable concordance of objective and subjective circumstances.

I would answer by saying that what confers on Arnim's work its particular intensity, and what seems liable to grant it from one moment to the next an entirely new exchange value, is that in some ways its determinations constitute the *geometric locus* of several highly serious conflicts, which since then have frankly only gotten worse. We must no doubt go all the way back to this work to find such ideal ground for the confrontation of some modes of thinking and acting that today are vying more violently than ever for human behavior. The unique aspect of this work is that, in it, the most exhilarating spiritual battle ever waged is simultaneously consumed and revived, in every guise that it might don in the course of a lifetime.

*   *   *

When Achim von Arnim turned twenty and was studying math and physics at the University of Göttingen, two scientific conceptions predominated – one of them of very recent vintage – which, rather than trying to be reconciled, maintained their antagonism at all costs and waged a life-or-death struggle against each other. Given the historical circumstances surrounding this debate, for a mind as agile and ardent as Arnim's no neutrality was possible. In order to make this understood, I must retrace the apparently singular ups and downs of the mental drama being played out at the time that, under the purely intellectual banner of imposing a choice between two methods (the experimental and the speculative), forces us to choose between two fundamentally discordant ways of explaining life and the world.

One cannot stress too highly the role physics played in the preoccupations of the Romantics. The skinned frog on Galvani's

table in 1786 that, contrary to expectation, performed the stacca-
to movement we all know about, could quite easily stand as their
poetic totem – keeping in mind the extraordinary revelation they
received from it, the help it gave them in perceiving a new world
immediately adorned with every mystic grace, and even the habit
they adopted, as if in its image, of wearing their hearts exposed.
It is remarkable that Arnim's own genius, when in 1800 he joined
the circle that had formed around the principal academics of
Jena, should point him toward Johann-Wilhelm Ritter. Taking
up from Galvani's experiments, and contemporaneously with
Volta (whose work he didn't know), Ritter had just shed light on
phenomena liable to confirm the discoveries of animal magnetism, and in general he indeed seems to be the most attractive
figure of the time. A physicist, but also an intriguer, theosophist,
and poet, Ritter was, as he himself recounts in the introduction
to his *Fragmente*, "afflicted with a bizarre tic, which took the
appearance of a mischievous 'spirit' and resembled almost exactly the 'automatic writing' of spiritualist mediums. This tic obliged him, at every moment, to interrupt himself in the very heat of
composition and write the most burlesque inventions in the mar-
gins of his manuscript."* This "Surrealist" before the fact
became, after Mesmer, the great apologist of sleep, by which, he
said, "man falls back into the universal organism, is physically
all-powerful," and becomes "a veritable magician." His attention was drawn to hypnotism, and particularly to somnambulism.
"In animal magnetism," he wrote, "one leaves the domain of
voluntary consciousness to enter into that of automatic activity,
into the region where the organic body behaves anew like an
inorganic being, and thus it *reveals to us the secrets of both worlds*

* E. Spenlé, *Novalis. Essai sur l'Idéalisme romantique en Allemagne.*

at the same time."* In order to have a more precise idea of his state of mind and the breadth of his experiments, we must also take into account the following declaration: "I have not been able to publish several of these fragments, because in their early form they appeared too daring and indecent – especially one of them, composed a few weeks before the author's marriage, of a kind that makes it seem impossible that a man with such ideas could ever think of marrying." It apparently concerned a story of sexual relations through the ages, with, in conclusion, a description of the ideal state of these relations – a description rendered in such terms, the author observes, "that this fragment would not have won clemency from even the most liberal judges, despite the rigor of its demonstration."** It is significant to find Achim von Arnim, whose first work was an "attempt at a theory of the phenomena of electricity," among the most assiduous guests of Ritter's country house in Belvedere, near Jena. It was there, they say, that fomented "a bias against Schelling," whose *Ideas Toward a Philosophy of Nature* was roundly attacked, Ritter choosing to see Schelling's system as a mere "fragment of Physics" and its author, incapable of being "a philosopher par excellence: a philosopher-chemist," as nothing more than a "philosopher-electrician."†

While several authors have mentioned close ties between Arnim and Novalis during this period, it seems that these were mainly due to the gratitude that supposedly bound Ritter to the poet, who had discovered him and removed him from his wretched living conditions. Indeed, despite his very frequent

* J.-W. Ritter, *Nachlass aus den Papieren eines jungen Physikers.*

** Spenlé, *Novalis, op. cit.*

† Xavier Léon, *Fichte et son temps.*

and highly suspect incursions into the metaphysical world, everything suggests that Ritter, as an experimenter of very high quality, would enjoy much greater respect from a young man such as Arnim – enamored of rigor (by training) and endowed with great curiosity (by temperament) – than would the mystical Novalis, who was deluded enough to blame Fichte for not having made *ecstasy* the basis of his philosophical system. Whatever the case, Novalis's death in 1801 put a very narrow time frame on any personal influence he might have had on Arnim. We also know that Arnim, who from the outset showed particular interest in the research of Priestly, Volta, and the physicist and humorist Lichtenberg, and whose Protestantism was strongly buttressed by Kantianism, maintained no personal contacts with Schelling. Having been among the first to condemn the *Philosophy of Nature*, he could not then follow its author through the vagaries of its evolution, or rally to his side when opportunism – which, the better to seduce Schelling, had donned the features of Caroline Schlegel – might have dictated his conversion to the murky ideas of Ritter and Jacob Boehme that pervaded the neo-Catholicism of the time. Similarly, we should note that he always kept his distance from the Schlegel brothers. Such an attitude, which I have every reason to believe was deliberate, implies that Arnim at that moment was an unabashed supporter of Fichte's theses, to the very large extent that, against constant and violent polemics, they defended the rights of Reason and Criticism, and espoused the philosophy of Reformation and Revolution. Lest there be any doubts about the clarity and vigor of his support, I need only cite a testimony that places in 1811, in other words the year that "Isabella of Egypt" was first published, a statement whose timing makes it all the more significant: "For more than one listener, student or not, Fichte's lectures, as

Achim von Arnim has remarked, filled the role once filled by Church religions."*

And so the remarkable situation created for the *mind,* which was openly being fought over by the opposing forces of progress and regression, managed (most likely with great effervescence and many second thoughts) to resolve itself in one of the best organized brains of the early nineteenth century, which we must not forget was essentially a poetic brain. A striking coalition – which, though unusually aware of its historical position, is perhaps no less eternal – groups together poets, artists, and scientists, who know all too well the price of the illumination that on rare occasions is produced through them; and knowing this, they cannot avoid deifying it and recognizing that something stands outside of it, even if this something is only darkness. From there, it is naturally just a short step to trying to broaden that darkness (as Schelling demonstrated when he attempted to win over the majority of Romantics to his philosophy), by preaching a return to mysticism and pledging science's allegiance to art, as he could not help doing when he stated that "both should meet and combine, were science to resolve all its problems, as art has *forever* [my emphasis] resolved its own."** In the other camp, assembled around the person of Fichte, as they would later be around Hegel, are the partisans of *Enlightenment*; and among these, as of that moment, it is essential that we recognize Achim von Arnim. This state of affairs, and it alone, allows us fully to grasp the remorse Clemens Brentano felt toward the end of his life – Brentano who ended up as a monk – when he blamed himself for having encouraged Arnim's marriage with his sister: "It was I,"

* Max Lenz, *Geschichte der Königl. Fr. W.*
** Schelling, *System of Transcendental Idealism.*

he says, "who led him to Bettina, whom I thereby delivered to literature, to the philosophers, to Young Germany. It is my fault that she lost her religion."

And it is again this conjuncture that explains why Arnim's work, which is nonetheless richer in fantasy than any other of the time, is in no way subject to the general reproach one might make against most German Romantic literature, which to my mind is expressed with incomparable decisiveness and authority in Hegel's judgment on *Heinrich von Ofterdingen,* the oh-so-nebulous novel by Novalis: "The young author has let himself be carried away by an initial brilliant invention, but he has not seen how defective such a conception is, precisely because it cannot be realized. The incorporeal figures and hollow situations are constantly shying away from reality, in which they should instead be resolutely engaged if they themselves are to claim any reality."* We find none of that arbitrariness, vagueness, and irresolution in Arnim. I am reassured, after having reread them many times, that he has not, in the course of these three novellas, committed the slightest abuse of confidence beyond putting into circulation and in relation creatures who are utterly free from the convention of presenting themselves, in their substance or their conduct, as realistic living beings. Once we accept their entrance on stage, these creatures behave with a naturalness and, we might say, a bravado that have no equivalent in the creations of any other storyteller. And in saying this, I am thinking in particular of Hoffmann and his two-bit "devils," including a supposed *golem* that comes in the wake of Arnim's and is nothing more than a vulgar counterfeit.** They are truly perfect objects of illusion, pushing flirtatiousness to the point

* Hegel, in *Jahrbücher für wissenshaftliche Kritik* [March 1828].

** P. Sucher, *Les Sources du Merveilleux chez E. T. A. Hoffmann.*

of apparently eluding the author's will, so that beside them, as if in avoidance of Romantic contagion, he seems an impersonal observer. The spectral side of some of these characters intentionally does not detract from their mood, which is sometimes excellent and leaves them free to romp about, to our great delight. In short, the speciousness of their existence does not at all prevent them, once they have been released into daily life, from manifesting their most valid penchants and from acting *logically* according to their own nature. I stress this all the more because nothing does Arnim more harm than to pass him off, as Heine and Gautier did, as a highly gifted inventor of horror stories. There are, moreover, many episodes of "Isabella of Egypt" that brilliantly contradict the claim (again by Heine and Gautier) of Arnim's imperturbable "seriousness" and of his fear of using specters too familiarly. To my mind, it would be totally vain for the reader to keep wondering whether any of these characters is really living or dead for Arnim, even when this uncertainty might procure in certain undemanding minds a pleasant feeling of panic. Once the first moment of emotion has passed, I believe it is far better to take his characters for what they are and very coldly observe that in their differences they do no more than reproduce, for instance, the properties of certain optical images that oscillate between virtuality and reality.

To my mind, in fact, this is the locus of Arnim's great secret, which is to bestow a very acceptable life onto certain inanimate figures, just as he gradually saps the life from creatures whose blood gave every appearance of circulating. Any reference to magic here would only obscure the problem and would poorly justify the noticeable part we play in these constant reversals of the hourglass. In Arnim's work, magic seems to be used merely as a backdrop, intervening only to facilitate in a wholly external manner the exhibition of a purely intellectual drama, which is the drama of German idealism at the beginning of the nineteenth century. Let us recall that the famous, decisive statement, "What is rational is real and what is real is rational,"* though not yet spoken or heard, was in the air by that time, and that any consciousness worthy of the name (as always happens in such cases) must have been somewhat aware of it. There nonetheless subsists, plain as day, Fichte's egregious error – which, let's not forget, was considered an error by none of the great Romantics, and which consisted in believing that *"thought* attributes being (objectivity) to sensation extended into space." I will point out that this way of conceiving the external world, which makes it depend solely on the power of the Ego and which is practically tantamount to negating it, opens the field very wide to possibilities of "externalization," even as it invites the mind to *decompose the movement that carries it toward that very externalization.* I mean by this that the Object, conceived as resulting from a series of efforts that progressively disengage it from nonexistence to bring it toward existence, and vice versa, in fact knows no stability between what is real and what is imaginary. This is quite clearly expressed by one of the characters in this book, the heir to the estate, when he declares, "I have difficulty distinguishing what I see with the eyes of reality *from what my imagination sees."* Moreover, the consideration of "secondary states" that we saw take a very active turn around Ritter tended to reinforce this ambiguity. Finally, artistic creation in the waking state, by the close ties it maintains with the unconscious creations of sleep and dream states, does not – and, it must be said, probably will never – allow for a total discrimination between these two solutions, the

* Hegel, *Principles of the Philosophy of Right.* [*trans.*]

real and the imaginary. The ambition of being a seer, of making oneself a SEER, began stirring in poets not with Rimbaud's formulation but with Arnim's – who, as early as 1817, proclaimed the identity of the two terms: *"Nennen wir die heiligen Dichter auch Seher"* [Let us call the sacred poets "seers"],* and who is perhaps the first to have completely realized it. For both of these poets, discovering in representation the mechanism of the imagination's operations and making the former depend solely on the latter has, of course, no meaning unless the Ego itself is subjected to the same regimen as the Object, unless a strict interdiction comes to shake up the "I am," which begins to lose itself in it. To my knowledge, it is in "The Heirs to the Estate" that, for the first time, a radical doubt is expressed toward such a statement, a logical doubt that rests on the possibility of abstracting the intuition of human internal activity from the action of thought that confers being; a doubt that, given the various states in which the Ego can be dispersed in the "external" object (particularly in childhood and in certain deliriums), consciously entails an overall disturbance of the notion of personality. Here again, instances of personality doubling, which Ritter observed in his own person, and experiments with telepathy and artificial somnambulism, which they would try out in Belvedere, seem to have lent a momentary appearance of concrete justification to Fichte's views and to have played a decisive role in the formation of Arnim's mind. For the record, I will simply allude to some of the stages crossed by that idea up to the present day, by citing Nerval's *Aurelia;* Rimbaud's philosophical profession of faith: "It's wrong to say: I think. Better to say: I am thought... *I* is an *other*"; Lautréamont's *Maldoror* and *Poésies*; Jarry's preconception of

* Introduction to *Guardians of the Crown* [*Die Kronenwächter*].

Caesar Antichrist with "places where everything is emblazoned, and certain persons doubled"; poems such as Nouveau's "Ignorant" or Apollinaire's "Procession"; and the entire opus of Salvador Dalí, in which, for example, the infinite multiplication of the oneiric image and the willful recourse to certain stereotypical effects radically compromise the objectifying power that, up until now, ultimately remained the province of memory. Even in the visual domain, Arnim could evoke the most lasting and modern disquiet, as when, a century before Picasso (and so many centuries after Apelles), he dreamed in "Isabella of Egypt" of a "canvas depicting fruits so skillfully rendered that birds, mistaking them for real fruits, flew up against the canvas."

Apart from this first conflict, whose repercussions are still considerable in our day – and to which the failure of subjective, then objective, idealism as a philosophy (or rather, their gradual absorption into dialectical materialism) has not put an end, on the level of either artistic creation or knowledge – Achim von Arnim's works still resound, albeit less strongly, with the clash of ideas in his day over the problem of the State, the choice of what organization to make socially predominant. The passably confused but ultra-reactionary doctrine that we find expressed simultaneously in Novalis's *Europe* and Schlegel's *Course of Lectures on Dramatic Art and Literature,* which can be contained in these four words: "mysticism, naturalism, Catholicism, Caesarianism," had originally had no adversary more dedicated than Fichte, whose rationalism, old democratic ideals, and, in a word, revolutionary spirit do not seem at any point to have suffered an eclipse. But it's precisely in these very convictions – which one might expect to be shared by Arnim, his passionate auditor – that a man might feel, not exactly shattered, but too strongly affected not to immediately react when an external factor, of the most brutal kind, comes along to annihilate his hopes for progress, his immediate will to perfection. We know that this ruinous, insurmountable factor was gratuitously and savagely inflicted on Enlightenment Germany by Napoleon in 1806. With him, the image of the man of Eighteenth Brumaire – whom the young German Romantics had had the weakness to see as a liberator, the man who would give France the "free government of a free nation" – toppled his full height. During the national awakening that followed in Germany thanks to Fichte, the aftershocks of which we are still feeling today (particularly after the latest adventure), it is possible that the French Revolution, too long identified with Napoleon, suffered enormous damage in the best of minds. It is undeniable that Arnim, in "Maria Melück-Blainville," proves exceedingly wary of it, and I can easily believe that, as legend has it, he later wholeheartedly supported the politics of von Stein. I would grant him the excuse that, for him as for others, the initial disappointment must have been too strong, the collapse of intellectual efforts too sudden, Germany's sudden poverty too great – and that Marx wasn't even born yet.

Still, in order for these objective causes of intellectual and moral agitation to be so forcefully expressed in Arnim's work, they had to have discovered more fertile ground in him than in anyone else; and for this to be so, *a priori*, some extremely dramatic events in Arnim's life must have kept him in a very peculiar emotional state. Indeed, it is not the least of the Romantics' honors to have recognized that the true possibilities of artistic genius lie only in the heart's shadow lands. I think that whoever opens this book, and after pondering its brilliance from every angle sees in it a marvelous thunder stone, will want to know what emotional storms engendered it.

I once had the opportunity to see some aerolites, which the ancient Aztecs cut so as to reveal a flat, circular, very dark surface, highly polished and reflective. They called these "love mirrors." In this case, cutting such a mirror would show us nothing more than the admirable face of Arnim next to the face of Bettina, she who has passed into German history under the name "the Child," and whom Goethe's mother saw as "the young woman with the firecracker imagination."

It was in 1801 that the two young people met, during a voyage that Bettina was taking with her brother Clemens Brentano, on which Arnim accompanied them, though apparently this first meeting did not bring them very close. After they parted company, in fact, the letters Clemens received from his friend glowed only with the poetic enjoyment he took in a peripatetic life, in the confident exchange of ideas, in the picturesque things encountered on the way; Bettina's existence had nothing to do with it, at least not overtly. For her part, the young woman, even while preserving the flowers that Arnim had given her, showered her brother with flattering missives in which she contrasted his own elegance and charm to Arnim's, who looked "so slovenly in his large overcoat with its frayed sleeves, with his goatskin flask, his hat with its ripped lining hanging out." Not until a few years later, during a second meeting in Frankfurt, did she sharply reverse the unfortunate impression that seems to have been caused above all by the poet's sartorial negligence. German anecdotal history retraces, with myriad details, the twists and turns of the night spent in a Frankfurt convent by Arnim, Brentano, Bettina, and her best friend, Karoline von Günderrode. Let me add, however, that we ought not complain of verbosity in this instance, as the story that has come down to us is a true breath of perfume. The summits of beauty, intelligence, and poetry seem to have dwelt for a few hours in that austere place. Karoline's personality even lends the scene a degree of mystery and depth that, in such an overflow of life, might otherwise be lacking. It seems that everything about the young canoness von Günderrode – she of the extremely gentle features, magnificent brown hair, light skin, bright blue eyes, and long, dark lashes; she who has been praised for her tall, willowy bearing under the heavy folds of her habit, her melodious glide when she walked, the moving expression of a summer's night promised, at rare intervals, only to the dawn of a laugh – would make her the focal point of the Romantic conception of women in its most stirring and bewildering aspects. It was she who, no doubt because she so feverishly incarnated the great contradictions of her day, soon afterward threw herself into the Rhine in Winckel, stabbing herself with a dagger at the same time. She and Bettina spent that night in Frankfurt sharing the very tender sentiments inspired in both of them by their discovery of Arnim's superior qualities. In their mutual exaltation, the two friends succumbed to an assault of generosity toward each other in which the poet's love was the stakes. It is possible, moreover, that the conversation was not entirely lost on him, since, according to Bettina, on several occasions he punctuated it from the adjoining room with a light cough, so much so that the next morning she avoided his eyes when he came to bring them flowers.

Whether or not he was put off by the childishness and daring of that double love declaration through the wall, Arnim saw no reason to follow it up, and according to him it was only in 1806, the year of Karoline's death, that his relationship with Bettina truly began. During that period, which was exceptionally unfortunate for Germany, he wrote to her of (and apparently sought her consolation for) his unhappy love affair with a certain

Augusta Schwinck, who by his own admission disdained him, whereas for him she was "like a patch of blue in the night sky above a battlefield." We should note that the sentence resorts to imagery only in its first words, as the poet would later stress when, to soothe any bitterness Bettina might have felt about it, he qualified that love as an "unreal passion during an unreal war." Moreover, we cannot entirely exclude a trace of artifice from the episode if we recall that Arnim later admitted having written to Bettina that at the time he was in love with *three* women, including herself and Augusta Schwinck, with the sole intention of provoking her spite, and in so doing "helping her to love him."

Whatever the case, it is important to note that 1807 was the year when the two young people discovered they were obviously infatuated with each other. Still, the four years that passed before their marriage would be, for Arnim, shot through with worries that one might normally assume to be entirely unjustified, but that, given all the precautions with which they are expressed, make us think that the man's pride and faith had been dealt a mortal blow.

I won't go so far as to ascribe to Bettina the inhuman courage that would let her systematically, and at Arnim's expense, match her acts to her words, namely, that genius comes into the world engendered by pain and prospers only in pain. Truth nonetheless obliges us to note that it was in 1807, in the month of April, that Bettina first visited Goethe and entered into extremely sustained relations with him for the next four years. While there can be no doubt about the platonic nature of these relations, Bettina, by later publishing her (greatly retouched) correspondence with the old man of Weimar,* leaves nothing to the imagination about her

---

* Bettina von Arnim, *Goethe's Correspondence with a Child.*

passionate feelings toward him. It is supremely disturbing to see this young woman – whose eyes are nonetheless as open to the world as can be, and whose voice in these letters still shivers from leaf to leaf with the most acute, spontaneous, and delicate accents that ever rang through the enchanted grove of sensitivity – to see this young woman let herself fall into the snare of glory. It is devastating to think that it was for Goethe, and not Arnim, that she unearthed all those marvels. We could find no other explanation for it but in the idea of a mission that haunted the minds of individuals such as Bettina or Karoline, who lived at the time in a state of high exaltation. For Goethe to surpass himself, or even to outlive his time – he who was losing the favor of a small German court, and who in 1808, in Erfurt, was pathetically flattered and flustered by Napoleon's welcome – could only mean that the "Child" he saw in Bettina deemed it necessary to give him the best of herself at that moment. I don't know just how desirable this was from a literary standpoint, and I admit finding it rather painful to learn that, toward the very end of his life, Goethe continued every day to open the drawer where he kept his letters from the last woman to "give him a glimpse of an admirable and charming picture book; she, the ravishing little dancer who with every movement spontaneously threw him a crown." The devil take that crown, I say, if I recall in addition Goethe's derisively partial, basely unsympathetic and hateful judgment about Arnim: "Nature, feminine; substance, chimerical; content, without consistency; composition, limp; form, floating; effect, illusory."* I do not share the common opinion that no excess is too great when singing a man's praises, and I cannot keep myself, before this famous *Correspondence*, of thinking of many flowers under a lot

* Goethe, *Würdigung's Tabelle der poetischen Produktion der letẓen Zeit.*

of ice. Nor is there anything there to accredit the idea of Bettina's love being shared between the addressee of these letters and someone else – moreover, I know of no such case of passionate doubling. Given this, I can only think that Arnim was suffering at the hands of the woman he loved more horribly than any man ever had, and that he was the victim of a veritable mystical betrayal.

Consequently, there is nothing of value in the testimony of Henri Blaze, who depicts Arnim's and Bettina's marriage in the romantic light he deems most favorable: "One day, Arnim was walking on Unter den Linden; Bettina passed by. Arnim was handsome as an angel... The *Child,* who never lowered her eyes when she walked, felt her head spin. With only her first impression to go on and in that resolutely impish tone... (etc.): 'You,' she said, staring at him with her fiery gaze, 'if you want me, I'll marry you.' Arnim smiled and their wedding was celebrated shortly afterward."* The reality, in many ways more prosaic, is that only after he came into an inheritance in 1810 could Arnim – who, as we have seen, had loved Bettina for quite some time – envision making her his wife; their betrothal became official on December 4 of that same year. Moreover, nothing could restore the atmosphere of that marriage better than a letter the poet sent to his friend Görres, dated April 14, 1811:

> So here I am a married man, a man of the interior with a kitchen, cellar, maid, and many domestic worries. But nowhere in the world is there a house more pleasantly nested than mine, in a large garden located in the middle of the city, shaded on one side by tall chestnut trees and poplars, on the other ringed

* H. Blaze, *Ecrivains et Poètes de l'Allemagne.*

by a rose garden – roses I planted myself. And if were to tell you now that my wife is Bettina Brentano, you'd understand how indifferent the French and the *Journal littéraire* have become to me, but that my friends and everything I once held so dear are still closest to my heart... You will surmise, without my having to prove it to you, that Bettina is the Unknown Woman to whom I dedicated *The Winter Garden*. And now she is mine, the Rhine is also mine, and I'm thinking of revisiting this summer all the paths and the heights I love so well.

The way we got married might amuse you, or at least amuse your wife, even if, thanks to the Nibelungen, she is half drowning in erudition. Five days after we got married in this city, without notifying either of our respective families, we went to tell Clemens and Savigny. You'll appreciate the difficulty when I say that I was living in the room next to Clemens's, while Bettina was living at Savigny's. But it so happened, as in a thousand comedies, that a chamber maid acted as intermediary for everything. Having secretly married that morning in the home of an octogenarian pastor, I went to Savigny's in the evening, as usual. I noisily tromped down the stairs, slammed the door to the house, and furtively turned back to Bettina's room, where she was joyously decked out in rosemary, jasmine, and myrtle. In the morning I left, telling Clemens that I had been so ill during the night that I had had to go to an inn, and at the same time I took a mild emetic that left no doubts on the subject. Why all these particulars, you ask? I'll answer in general: because of gossip; and especially because of gossip about Clemens, which disturbs him more and more as he begins to get out in society. But generally speaking because every exceptional marriage, as ours inevitably was, is subject to the most annoying derision of any sacrament, to the most grievous ribaldry, even if people also feel obligated to shed a few tears.

Given these last remarks, we might well suppose that Arnim was not admitting the true cause of his apprehension or, who knows, that he didn't dare admit it to himself. I don't think the annals of emotional life can reproduce anything that, though cloaked in triumph and the dazzle of festive songs, would surpass the cruelty of this situation: "Can one imagine," says Blaze, "this husband, this poet whose wife is known the world over — not because of him, a great and noble mind whom the crowds ignore, but through her ecstatic hymns intoned at the altar of another great poet?"* And if we think that the year 1817, which with the publication of *Guardians of the Crown* surely marked the high point of Arnim's genius, was also the one in which, at home, the unbelievable canticle to Goethe started up again: can one imagine (I would add) a disaster such as this love, a love attacked so unnaturally at its very roots, which hides instead of blazing out in broad daylight like a paragon, which hides like a sickly weed? So many precautions: the almost immediate break between the newlyweds and the Goethe household, their retreat to the country home at Wiepersdorf, where soon it became hard to tell which of them felt more abandoned and less adapted to their new life, with its numerous children... all this to end up at the total negation of Bettina writing to the man of sixty-eight: "If the enclosed leaf has retained its color, you will see what color my love is for you. It seems to me that it is still bright red, solid, and dotted with gold dust. Your bed is made in my heart. Please do not spurn it!" To the man of seventy-two: "Ten years of solitude have passed

* H. Blaze, *Les Ecrivains modernes de l'Allemagne.*

through my heart and have separated me from the source where I drew life. Since then, I have stopped using the same words; everything I felt and hoped has faded... Love is not an error; but, alas! error pursues it." To the man, again, of seventy-four: "At the midnight hour, surrounded by memories of my youth, having behind me all the sins you wish to accuse me of and that I completely admit, before me the heaven of reconciliation, I seize the nocturnal goblet and empty it to your well-being, and seeing the dark color of the wine on the lip of the crystal, I think of your beautiful eyes."

These days, the sexual world, despite the memorable explorations made in the modern age by Sade and Freud, has never, as far as I can see, stopped countering our will to penetrate the universe with its unshatterable kernel of *darkness*. Subjectivity, which one morning immobilized beneath the willows the corpse of the beautiful Günderrode, a towel full of stones knotted about her neck – just as it sank the boat in which two unique individuals had so harmoniously (or so it seemed) taken their seats – continues to cradle and topple our most cherished calculations with its inexorable refrain. Far be it from me to speak ill of subjectivity, moreover, since one of the greatest human defeats it ever inflicted led to the publication in 1822 of the final tale in this book, which lets us situate concretely one pole of the mental ecliptic, in opposition to the realistic, conception of things. To the extent that Goethe's final thought can be taken as an oracle, namely, that the Eternal Feminine is truly the cornerstone of the entire edifice, we can still expatiate today upon the fact that this oracle took Bettina as its sibyl, though in opposite ways for Goethe and Arnim. Ritter mysteriously claimed that man, a stranger on the earth, is acclimated here below only by woman. He merely "delivers" woman, helps her discover her purest destination. It's the earth that, in some way, gives its orders through woman. "We love only the earth, and through woman the earth loves us in return." This is why love and women are the clearest solution to every enigma. "Know woman, and the rest will follow on its own."

It will soon be one hundred years since Arnim died...

1933

Picasso in His Element

T HAT ORDINARY BUTTERFLY, forever immobilized next to a dry leaf: for an entire afternoon I kept wondering how it could confer such particular importance on the little canvas I'd been looking at that morning in Picasso's studio, so that the objects I turned to afterward – objects I had nonetheless always loved above all others – seemed freshly illuminated. I kept wondering how its perfect incorporation into the painting could suddenly provoke in me the unique emotion that, when it seizes us, is the incontrovertible witness to our having just been granted a revelation. Although Picasso's work, for those who know how to see, has always been one of the primary places in our epoch where such a revelation has the most consistent chance of occurring, it behooves us – so as not to diminish our sense of the necessity, harmony, and strength of this work – to delight for a moment in contemplating those sparkling patches through which the radiant river sings of its triumph over the obstacle it had set itself.

What a marvelous, irresistible current! To all those who refuse to see in Picasso anything more than a desire to astonish, who persist (some gratefully, others less so) in taking an external view of his audacities alone, I'll never stop making a case for the admirable *moderation* of thought that has never obeyed anything but its own extreme tension. In 1933, for the first time, a butterfly straight out of nature alit in the field of a painting, and could do so without everything around it instantly falling into dust, without the overwhelming emotions aroused by its presence harming the system of human representations in which it was included. As such, this system, which is Picasso's alone, once again demonstrates its genius. It seems to me that the total assimilation of a real animal organism into a figurative mode that can boast of having broken with every conventional mode would alone be enough to silence its detractors, to confound all those who, disingenuously or not, persist in challenging it. Yet here is the proof. The limits assigned to expression are exceeded once more. A delicate magnetic blood spreads copiously over the ravishing white basin, no wider than a hand. Everything that is subtle in the world, everything we can know reaches that spot only gradually: the passage from the inanimate to the animate, from objective to subjective life – whether animal, vegetable, or mineral – finds its most surprising resolution here, reaches its most mysterious and sensitive unity From this previously unattained point, we may consider a bit haughtily the belated child's play of so-called artistic "realism," which is blinded by the *appearance* of things, and which brings universal chemistry to a halt – without offering anything to see – just when painters fill their color pots.

In a jumble, treated no differently from the other work materials lying next to them in his studio, or even from the floor that no one makes any effort to keep neat or shiny, these pots are there for strictly practical reasons, at the disposal of a man who is no longer concerned with the unconditional reproduction of the colored image (the painter at parrot school) but rather with the reconstitution of the world, starting with the idea that form demands to be posed as neutral and indeterminate, as *free* – through his stroke – and that only afterward arises the possibility of individualizing it to the extreme by introducing an indifferent substance: in other words, color. And even if merely looking at it from a corner of one's room isn't enough to make you think so, it's clear that Picasso has no bias toward color. As he once confessed to Edouard Tériade: "How many times, just as I was about to add some blue, did I notice that I didn't have any! So I took some red and added it instead."* Because the fact is, blue and red, for anyone essentially preoccupied with exploring the realm of physical matter, cannot be conceived as anything other than particular states – which are practically negligible in their particularity – of this individualizing and concretizing principle of color, a unity of light and dark obtained by the mediation of transparency. Color taken as a general thing, without its scale of differentiation, through the reciprocal limitations of light and darkness that it translates, is above all able to fill with reality the emptiness left by form, visually highlighting the real physical object, guaranteeing its existence at every point. That this object *should be* is more important than knowing it will give the impression of a sky or of blood. Let's recall the Bohemian crystal wine glass whose inner edge Goethe had covered half with white paper, half with black, so that the glass appeared blue and yellow. To my mind, no domain is more imbued with relativism, all the more so since any analysis of a pigment leads indistinctly to metal, and variations in color imply only certain differences in density from one metal to another. That's why we can only feel sorry for those who, claiming to like or understand Picasso's painting, find his beige and gray period (from 1909 to 1913) rather arid. To get a real grasp of this concrete and external existence of things, it is thrilling to think how a man deprived himself for several years running of all the spellbinding and dangerous powers dormant in metal, when these powers had so ideally rushed to his aid in the ten preceding years. And yet one day Picasso silenced

* E. Tériade, "En causant avec Picasso. Quelques pensées et réflections du peintre et de l'homme," *L'Intransigeant* (June 5, 1932).

the great organ music in him, and trying to capture the murmur of the most secret spring, set out to meet the entire forest. Dear gray paintings, where everything finishes and begins afresh, like those roofs that the painter sees from his window, slanting beneath the great veil of the Parisian sky with its changing clouds. The same light smoke, scarcely a shade brighter or darker than this sky (depending on the hour), is alone enough to evoke human life by stages and sections: women shaking out their hair before a mirror, flowers blooming on the wallpaper – life at once bitter and full of charm. The painterly instinct, which here is brought to the summit of its individual development, takes from the refusal, the negation of everything that could distract it from its own signification, the means to reflect upon itself. A will to total consciousness, which has entered here for perhaps the first time, gives meaning to the effort, illuminating the laborious process that from the lowest to the highest echelon of the animal species lets a living being use a dwelling, weapon, trap, or mirror. Picasso will meet all these needs, will perform all these experiments in disintegration with implacable lucidity. In one single being who is gifted and eager to understand all others, the spider, by some miracle, will be more attentive to the pattern and substance of the polygon of its web than to the fly, the migratory bird will turn toward what it is leaving, just as it will try to find itself in the labyrinth of its own song. In this point where artistic creation – whose goal is to affirm in each being the hostility animating his desire toward the external world – finally renders the external object adequate to this desire, and thereby to some extent reconciles that object with the external world, it was crucial to install an instrument precise enough simply to register the dialectical movement of the mind, beyond any objective consideration of final agreement or disagreement. We should not forget that such a work must be considered the product of a particular *excretion;* only secondarily can we ask whether its immediate appearance is apt to contribute to human happiness. The criterion of taste would moreover prove itself derisory were we to apply it to Picasso, whose works have both marvelously pleased and displeased. More important, in that it alone suggests a man's revolutionary power to make the world conform to his desires (and is therefore wholly revolutionary), is the uninterrupted attempt to confront what exists with what might exist; to bring out of the never-seen whatever can push the already-seen to be perceived less carelessly. The most elementary spatial relations are grasped by whoever is familiar with Picasso's apartment and has walked with him from room to room, with unparalleled acuity and avidity. Let a pile of abandoned cigarette packs on a mantelpiece, with its irregular and meaningless whirl of red and white stickers, arbitrarily form a pair (a pair such as to plunge the spirit of arrangement and bourgeois luxury into eternal despair) with a plaster figure surrounded by some absurd multicolored vase, and suddenly the whole mystery of human and animal construction is at stake. A rising stack of boxes takes on the importance of a problem solved somewhere in the night of time: the statue is only the solution to a current problem, with its own greater or lesser complexity. Just let these figures, those armored iron objects stand elsewhere, shoulder-to-shoulder with bottles of gas or varnish, and their impalpable volume clearly appears next to the other, palpable ones. Life itself then becomes, or is, part of their total transparency; the philter of life itself stretches them from one metal stem to another. Yet it is quite clear that they must come to us mainly as signals, that they would be deceptive were they to attract our attention in isolation, causing us to lose everything that matters: in other words, the interminable gestation taking place through them. In Picasso's life and person, this gestation appears in a series of *optimal* moments: we cannot forget that it began and must continue beyond them. This will be true until knowledge manages to encompass all of natural necessity, which still escapes human laws and points up their narrowness, haste, and fallibility. Given that the great enigma, the permanent cause of the conflict between man and the world, resides in the impossibility of justifying everything by logic, how could one ask the artist or scientist to justify the ways that imperious human need chooses to satisfy itself by setting external things *against* other external things, in which the entire resistance of the internal being is at once given up and included? Picasso is great in my eyes precisely because he has constantly remained on the defensive against these external things, including those he had drawn from himself, and has never taken them to be anything but *moments* of intercession between himself and the world. He has sought out the perishable and the ephemeral for themselves, going against the grain of everything that is usually the object of artistic delight and vanity. The twenty years that have washed over them have already yellowed those newspaper clippings, whose fresh ink contributed their fair share to the insolence of his magnificent collages from 1913. The light has faded, and humidity has stealthily lifted the corners of the great cutouts in blue and pink. And that's the way it should be. The stupefying guitars made of low-grade wood, makeshift bridges cast daily over the song, have not held up against the singer's headlong rush. But it's as if Picasso had already counted on this impoverishment, this weakening, even this dismembering. As if in this unequal struggle waged *nonetheless* by human creations against the elements, where there is no doubt about the outcome, he had wanted in advance to leave his options open, to reconcile everything precious (because ultra-real) with the process of its wasting away. Thus the stag-beetle, flying in oak forests on stormy June evenings with its face to the sun, despite its marvelous covering like that of some black prince, and after a hatching period lasting four or five years, enjoys no more than a month of existence in the open air – the same open air that the crow's piteous caw pierces for a hundred years. If there is room in nature for two beings presenting such an analogy of color, an opposition of structure, and a paradoxical difference in life span, it seems to me that a work of art should take it into account; that the artist, whose primary concern is to create a living thing, can do no less before attempting it than to weigh a bird feather against an insect's wing-sheath. I exult in the fact that while certain of Picasso's paintings take their solemn place in the museums of the world, he still makes ample room for everything that will never become an object of admiration or speculation of any sort other than intellectual. In this, too, the conception he has of his own work can seem absolutely dialectical. Now is the time to underline this, at the moment when a journal is gathering and presenting a large portion of his recent *extra-pictorial* production. A common plant – a fig tree, for instance – serves here not only as support but also as *justification* for an iron sculpture that is inseparable from it in the observer's mind. The sculpture is subjected to the same fate as the fig tree. So true is this that one can see that another image has deserted the area around the dead fig tree, whose roots spring from the earth, arch over, and mingle inextricably in a supreme convulsion, the grimace of an embrace. The total lignification of the stem, sheathed at its end with an animal horn; the absence of leaves compensated, in contrast, by the imperceptible trembling of a little red feather, are exploited in contradiction to anything that could possibly arouse a feeling of the real life of the bush. But this same idea of support or backing, with all the (once again) justificative value that clings to it, this idea reflecting upon itself demands reciprocity: if the sculpture is based on the plant, it is just as valid for extremely disparate objects to be based on it as well (so it is of dubious interest to wonder whether ivy was made for the wall, or the wall for ivy). In and of themselves, these objects – the cap of a street corner vizier, the little "Mickey Mouse" or the *marmosets* of local fairs, cheap toys – will never be too humble or too futile to attack the dignity of this cast-iron personage, who seems never to know what to do with his foot – which moreover is just a metal cobbler's mold. For anyone who would still feel entitled to cast doubt on the dialectical progression of that thought, I think it will be enough to point out how, during his exhibit last June at the Georges Petit galleries, Picasso placed on opposite sides of a long room two great ironworks – one of which seemed covered with rust and the other freshly coated with white paint – showing quite clearly that with their extremely dissimilar coverings he wanted the two to *answer each other* as visitors passed by. These two statues, twins beyond any doubt, exchanged all the remarks of a lightly ironic philosophy, remarks that become apt the moment one lets oneself raise the problem of fate.

If, as we have seen, Picasso the painter has no bias toward color, we might expect that Picasso the sculptor would not have any bias toward matter. Indeed, with a meaningful and charming complicity, he draws our attention to the slight imperfections that the frail creatures he invents, which come gilded from the foundry, draw from their original substance: some slip of the chisel, a few accidents in the wood. In his hands, moreover, these imperfections undeniably become so many visible perfections. Wood, wire, or plaster are used here one serially or together, by a man whose need for concretization is instantly renewed by its very gratification; a man who is, like all great inventors, continually prey to others' requests; for whom it is totally useless and, no doubt, totally impossible to see anything ahead of time. An elective attraction, excluding any previous elaboration, alone determines – through substances found literally *at hand* – the appearance of a body or a head. This matter is nevertheless cherished for itself, but only like matter in general, completely outside any consideration of its particular states. It is cherished as in Rimbaud's "Feasts of Famine":

> If I've a taste, it is alone
> For eating simply earth and stone.
> Dinn! dinn! dinn! dinn! So let us dine
> On air, and rock, and coal, and iron.

But, you may ask, why plaster as well? Why should we still be served up all that classic porridge of plaster? A chorus of young voices gathers around me, fascinated and irritated, shouting: enough plaster! The greedy Picasso has better things to do than ruin all that plaster! But I fear it is really *their* dialectical sense and not his that falls short. Since the external object, as I've tried to define it visually, is produced by the principle of darkness manifested in bright light, it is measured on the surface by color; so when it occurs in a three-dimensional mass, deprived of any support from color, it tries to make up for it by showing the appropriate relation of shadow to light. This relation does not require us to ponder that object *in a static position* – which would mean having to walk absurdly around the object to assure ourselves of its existence. Picasso was very explicit on the subject as early as 1906, when he painted his famous women with "noses shaped like a wedge of Brie," those faces seen both frontally and in profile where people liked to point out the preponderance of a sculptor's concerns. Of course it is ideally through the mediation of the docile and immaculate substance of plaster that these relations of shadow and light, implying all the quantitative shifts in volume – nothing in common with expressionist "distortions" – can be perceived in the infinite possibility of their variation. A real object: a head, a body whose light patches would replace shadows, and vice versa... perhaps that's the extreme case, but we'd still like to see it. To be able to reflect on the self in the work of art, not only knowing oneself to be other than oneself, but in wanting, in tolerating the contrary of oneself... Picasso now delights in building these mental snowmen.

If these denser white human forms, more immediate in appearance, should seem to some eyes colder and more ephemeral, I think it merely a lack of adjustment, or some recurrence of the absurd and not always well-intentioned concern that you hear so often about Picasso: what if he were suddenly to return to direct imitation; if he were just to forgo the whole disquieting, adventurous, revolutionary part of his undertaking; if he were to settle back into normality, consenting to be exactly what he was (*with such brio!*) every time he tried it, a representational artist! I've no reason to belabor how shabby an attack is lurking in these words, what little faith they show in the solidity of the principles that so wonderfully inform a living man, in full consciousness and full pride, and at the vanguard of exploring the physical world. A few days ago, in Picasso's studio, I was leafing through his long, recent series of admirable etchings that seemed to record, hour after hour, the meaning and the development of his last venture. This strictly intellectual venture is there, deliberately commented on in actual life. The last, light veils that, to the observer, always seem to protect every particular artistic creation from complete nakedness fall one by one before this *sculptor's parable.* In them one can see the artist moving about under his antique mask, Jupiter-like; his long gaze coming and going from the eternal female model, *whom he takes the time to caress,* to the block of matter in which all the infinite possibilities of representation are inscribed; or else it wanders outside to a tender curve of valleys, in the dazzle of the purest sky. The eye, while following with delight from one engraving to the next, I should say – from one state of engraving to the next – the prodigiously varied spectacle appearing on this stand, recognizes how it undergoes such a metamorphosis. The heads appearing upon these pages that we turn one after the other, these heads and many others – some of them resembling the complex systems of lenses used for lighthouses – reveal, beyond the surprise of their apparent diversity, the secret of their *unity.* Their vital, organic link can be measured by the normality of what continues to happen beside them, and this is very simple, very human: just now the woman's hand was rising toward the magnificent beard, now it's the man lifting high between his fingers the sparkle of a small glass bowl where a fish is swimming. Like all the lovely gestures that give life its charm, these can never be premeditated. The engraving tool, running over the copper, suddenly finds itself dreaming up a new relation between these two beings, introducing the little fish for a few seconds of pleasure.

A spirit so constantly and so exclusively inspired is capable of turning everything to poetry, ennobling everything. It is created to stand in extreme opposition, to cause instant failure to the somber intentions of all those who, for unspeakable reasons, try to oppose man to himself and who for that reason are always on the watch, lest through some weakness he should escape the nauseating disquiet that dualistic thought provokes and encourages. Among a quantity of paintings and objects that Picasso showed me the other day, each more dazzling than the last in their freshness, intelligence, and liveliness, there appeared a tiny unfinished canvas, of the same size as the one with the butterfly, whose center contained only a thick patch of paint. Making sure it was dry, he explained to me that the subject of this canvas was to be a little pile of excrement, which would be apparent when he placed a few flies around it. He was only sorry that he had to use color to compensate for the lack of some real dried excrement, the *inimitable* sort that you find in the countryside in the season when children eat cherries without bothering to remove the pits. His choice of these pits in this place seemed, I must say, to bear the most objective witness to the very special interest that should be paid to the relation between what is unassimilated and what is assimilated, in which variations in meaning for the sake of the human can be seen as the essential goal of artistic creation. Any slight repugnance aroused by the thought of this single spot, around which the painter's magic was only beginning to take effect, was more than overcome by that. I was surprised to find myself imagining those glittering flies, all new as Picasso would know how to make them. Everything took on a new delight; not only did my gaze not remember having rested on anything disagreeable, but more than that I was *elsewhere*, in good weather, where living was pleasant, among the wild flowers and the dew: I plunged freely into the forest.

June 1933

The Faces of Women*

F AIR FACES GATHERED OUTSIDE OF TIME, faces of living women, I am seated on a bench in springtime, dreaming of a passing tram, the color of mist rising from the
meadow, with a lovely head at each window. Everything that the
most beautiful street in the world at the most beautiful moment
cannot offer, is freely invited here to set down its luminous streak.
The most beautiful street in the world? Better today's than
never's. Not in vain have the night's neons mingled their fiery letters with the hair of dark violets or pearls. The breath of those
low-slung cars might have nibbled, once and for all, these long
manes of hair, ready to curl just a little below the ear, eager to
flutter off at the slightest movement. The ear that they alternately cover and reveal is not quite the same either, since it has been
awaiting someone to summon it from some other place, from any
other point in the world liable to annihilate this one. I won't even
try to say what these eyes have seen, which is invisible for others
– what in them, therefore, generally holds me captive. No matter,
it is clear that they burn brighter not only because they unconsciously reflect human existence at what for us is, and will remain,
its final stage – the sciences, the arts, all the various means of
seduction: fashion, philosophies, the present state of morals – but
above all because our own eyes are burning with just the same
fire, are just as likely to be enchanted, dazzled, tear-filled before
these eyes. These nostrils are trembling, these lips moving, these
breasts heaving; a whole community of scents, thoughts, and

* Preface to the album *Man Ray*, 1934.

breath attaches us to these beings as to no others, makes us aware once more of the best we have known: the arousal of our heart in the very heart of this century. These marvelously instinctive poses are the ones they were the first to strike; each one of them is a gathering of desires and dreams that had never been assembled before and will never be again. Shadow and light, in the repose and the silence of a few seconds, have served to shape these perfect incarnations, both of everything most modern in poetry, music, and dance and in what is eternally most youthful in the art of love.

Only from Man Ray could we have expected the true "Ballad of the Ladies of Time Present," of which we can give only an extract here. What a challenge, is it not, to try to surprise human beauty at just the moment when it truly takes on its full power: so sure of itself that it can seem unconscious! It took this great hunter's eye, this patience, this sense of the pathetically just moment when the balance, of the most fleeting kind, is glimpsed in an expression, caught between dreaming and action. It took nothing less than this admirable experience that is Man Ray's, in the widest visual domain, to try, beyond any immediate resemblance – which all too often is only that of a day or certain days – to aim at the deepest resemblance involving everything one might become, physically and morally. The portrait of someone you love should be not only an image at which you smile but also an oracle you question. It finally took all the sparkling curiosity, all the flawless audacity that always characterizes Man Ray's intellectual procedures, for there to arise, from so many contradictory and charming traits that he chooses to offer us, the unique being in which we can see the latest avatar of the Sphinx.

October 1933

The Automatic Message

O H NO NO I'M BETTIN' on Bordeaux Saint-Augustin...
That's a notebook, that is." [*Oh non non j'parie
Bordeaux Saint-Augustin... C'est un cahier ça.*] At
around eleven P.M. on September 27, 1933, while trying to fall
asleep a bit earlier than usual, I take down one of those phrases
spoken – once again without any conscious provocation on my
part – as if from nowhere but perfectly clearly, and forming (to
what we commonly call our "inner ear") a remarkably coherent
whole. I have tried on several occasions to highlight these particular verbal groupings that, taken individually, might seem rich or
poor in significance, but that, by the suddenness of their passage
and their utter lack of hesitation in coming together, offer the
mind too exceptional a certainty for us not to study them very
closely. Man, caught up by day in his morass of clichés, comes to
conceive of all things, including himself, through a dizzying
series of slips that he immediately conceals, of false steps that he
rectifies as best he can. To counter his fundamental imbalance,
civilized modern man turns more and more to a vain and artificial
concern with minimal, transitory balances: the written page is lit-
tered with odious cross-outs, which like a line of rust cancel out
life itself. All those "sonnets" that are still being written, all the
senile horror of spontaneity, all the rationalistic refinement, all
the conceit of supervisors, all that inability to love only serve to
convince us that we can never escape the decrepit house of cor-
rections. To correct, correct *oneself*, polish, revise, rewrite, rather
than to dip blindly into one's subjective treasures simply for the
pleasure of scattering on the table a handful of frothing algae and

emeralds: such is the order that poorly understood rigor and slav-
ish prudence (in art and elsewhere) have bent us to for centuries.
Such, too, is the order that has been countermanded on a few rare
but critical occasions. Surrealism derives from that.

In 1816, Herschel manages to obtain within himself the
"involuntary production of visual impressions, into which geo-
metrical regularity of form enters as the leader character, and
that, under circumstances which altogether preclude any explanation drawn from a possible regularity of structure in the retina or
the optic nerve... If it be true," he says, "that the conception of
a regular geometric pattern implies the exercise of thought and
intelligence, it would almost seem that in such cases as those
above adduced we have evidence of a *thought,* an intelligence,
working without our own organization distinct from that of our
own personality." Eyes wide open in a dark room, Watt conceives
the future, the *next* steam engine. What is not yet will be. Inside
a simple crystal ball, like the kind used by soothsayers, one man
or one woman out of twenty, they say – but have the nineteen
others understood what this means? can we entirely absolve them
of any unconscious ill will? – manages after a few minutes (and
on condition that he or she remain in a state of mental passivity)
to see a more or less disturbing object emerge, a scene unfold
whose actors are more or less familiar, etc.

I think one must never have been alone, never have taken time
to submit to the marvel of hope that consists in conjuring from
total absence the real presence of a loved one, not to have (at least
hypothetically) run one's longing gaze over that supremely
anonymous and unreasonable object: the crystal ball, empty
in daylight but harboring everything in darkness. A tear, that
masterpiece of crystalloscopy... The expression "Everything is
written" must, I believe, be taken strictly literally. Everything is

written on the blank page, and when writers go for something like a revelation or a *photographic* development, they are merely indulging in vain mannerisms. True, I neglected to mention that they put something of themselves into it – and a very poor something it is, since this "of themselves" is in reality *of others*. I'm tempted to say instead that they take something of themselves *out* of it, to put in something empty. As people are fond of saying, Leonardo Da Vinci recommended that his students stare fixedly at a crumbling old wall to find artistic subjects. "Before long," he told them, "you will see shapes and scenes begin to emerge with increasing clarity... At that point, you need only copy what you see, and complete it if need be." But no matter how often it gets mentioned, the fact is that the lesson has been lost. The beautiful interpreting wall, all crackled, now leans like a mere fence post over speeding traffic, before which an unformed landscape reconstitutes the magic mirror in which life and death can be read. Let's waste no time on regrets. Rather – no objections from me – let us gaze with heartfelt gratitude at these elementary surfaces in which the world to come has tried for so long to take form. Coffee dregs, melted lead, fogged mirror: it is still from you that these impenetrably clear women's veils are made. That man in the restaurant isn't waiting for anyone; he's taking a great interest in his congealed partridge sauce. That other one, lighting his cigar, doesn't realize he is smoking visions.

To come back to the poetically disappointing quote that began these pages, what mainly drew my attention to it was the surprise I felt at its childlike intonation. The "Oh" with its very open vowel sound and the marked lisp in the second sentence, in that *absence of sound* that characterizes the "inner voice," did not (as I immediately noted) permit me to attribute the statement to any particular child, except that it was a little boy. Moreover, no visual or other kind of representation was associated with it. My observation of this fact, insignificant in itself, seems worth reporting only insofar as it differs from and, to some extent, contradicts my earlier statements. In the first and second *Manifesto of Surrealism* I used only examples of *silent phrases* (so to speak), which I cited without quotation marks because the personality expressed in them so closely matched my own personality of the moment: these phrases had always seemed readily adaptable to my voice, without my having to disguise them in any way. The question of "verbal impulse" (much like "graphic impulse") is, by the psychologists' own admission, so complex; can be posed so differently for each different individual; and can be considered so important in so many ways, that anyone who believes he can broaden our knowledge of this field, even minutely, should tell us everything he can on a daily basis. We know, in fact, that this enigma – also called "the enigma of intellectual locution" or of "intellectual vision" – dominates the entire problem of hallucinations in clinical medicine, just as in philosophy it challenges the reality of the external world, and, in the artistic sphere as it currently stands, accredits the idea of "genius."

As to the matter of genius, it is undeniable that the poetic and visual output of the past ten years has only exacerbated this feeling of ambiguity. If Surrealism's efforts have tended above all to bring inspiration back into favor, and if, in so doing, we have exclusively promoted the use of automatic forms of expression; if, on the other hand, psychoanalysis has managed beyond all expectation to give a penetrable meaning to the kinds of improvisations that people had heretofore labeled gratuitous, conferring upon them (without regard for aesthetic concerns) a considerable value as human documents, we must still admit that not enough light has been shed on the conditions under which an "automatic" text or drawing should be produced, in order to be completely valid.

Before getting to this, I must point out that the growing curiosity attached these days to manifestations of automatic thought can only be read as a sign of the times, by which I mean that it indicates a widespread feeling of need, at least for the early twentieth century. Very often, today's young writers and artists have eagerly proclaimed their strict filiation to Lautréamont and Rimbaud – and indeed, in the context of automatism, we can speak of a veritable *watchword* that these two poets, *who both proved to be implacable theoreticians,* passed down to us. In a wholly different vein, some of us ascribe to Charcot – whose teaching (dogmatic though it may have been) inaugurated the magnificent and still ongoing debate on hysteria – the responsibility for a large part of the research that takes its cue from such poets. (To Dr. von Schrenck-Notzing goes the honor of having stressed the "artistic value of movements of expression in hysteria and hypnosis," at the first International Conference on Psychology in Paris, 1889.) I believe, moreover, that despite the regrettable ignorance that many still have of his work, we are much more indebted than we realize to what William James rightly called the *gothic psychology* of F. W. H. Myers, who predated Freud, and who, in an entirely new and fascinating context, later enabled Théodore Flournoy to conduct his admirable explorations. It is hardly worth stressing the fact that, as much as we are interested in resolving the problem of granting (artistic) exchange value to a given form of undirected expression, or in the role of (moral) compensation filled by automatism, we are at least equally interested in resolving what the same William James called the (strictly psychological) *Myers problem.* This problem was, and still is, to determine the precise constitution of the subliminal. I repeat that we are now faced with a veritable sheaf of demands that, intellectually, can be said to express the needs endemic to our era. Like it or not, the time has passed for us to take any interest in the "beautiful" and "clear" organization of so many works that rely merely on the superficial, conscious level of being. It is possible that the violent economic and social contradictions of recent years have had everything to do with the depreciation of this paltry jewel.

The history of automatic writing in Surrealism – and I'm not afraid to say it – is one of continual misfortune. Indeed, not even the underhanded protests of the critics, who have been particularly attentive and hostile on this point, will keep me from recognizing that, for years, I counted on the torrential outpouring of automatic writing to cleanse the literary stables definitively. In this regard, the desire to throw open the floodgates will certainly remain the generative idea of Surrealism. It says something that, in my eyes, the movement's partisans and adversaries will always and easily be defined by whether they value only the authenticity of the automatic product or whether, on the contrary, they wish to see it reconciled with something other than itself. Quality, here as elsewhere, could not help becoming a function of quantity. If there was no lack of quantity, some easily imagined factors kept it from acting on the public scale as a force of submersion: thousands of notebooks, *each as good as the next,* have remained in desk drawers. The important thing, moreover, is for more such notebooks to be filled, an infinite number – and better still, for their authors frequently to compare their method with ours and to admit to us openly their technical concerns.

Although I never sought to codify the ways in which this highly personal and infinitely variable dictation was obtained, I have not been able to avoid (by suggesting certain modes of behavior) simplifying the *listening* conditions to an extreme degree, nor generalizing totally individual methods of resumption in case the current was interrupted. I also omitted, even in a series of publications that came after the first *Manifesto,* to specify the nature of the obstacles that often conspire to divert the verbal outflow from its original direction. Whence the very legitimate questions – which furthermore did not meet the slightest objection – that I have sometimes been asked: How can one ensure the homogeneity or remedy the heterogeneity of the constituent parts of such a discourse, which often seems to contain scraps of several discourses? What should one make of interferences or gaps? How can one keep from visualizing up to a certain point what is being said? How can one tolerate the distressing passage from the auditory to the visual? etc. It is unfortunately quite true that up until now, those who dipped "poetically" into automatic writing have not all been equally concerned with such questions. Many, in fact, have preferred to see automatic writing only as a new science of literary *effects,* which they blithely adapted to the needs of their little industry. I believe I can say that the automatic flux, which they had flattered themselves they could use at their leisure, lost no time in abandoning them completely. Others spontaneously contented themselves with a half-measure that consists in encouraging the eruption of automatic language in the midst of more or less conscious developments. Finally, we must note that numerous pastiches of automatic texts have recently been put into circulation – texts that are not always easy to distinguish at first glance from authentic examples, because we lack objective, original criteria. These obscurities, these failings, these stagnations, these efforts at simulation seem to demand more imperiously than ever, for the benefit of the actions we mean to carry out, a complete *return to first principles.*

A precise distinction must be established between "automatic" writing and drawing, in the sense that the term is used in Surrealism, and automatic writing and drawing as they are commonly practiced by mediums. The latter – those of them, at least, who truly have remarkable abilities – set down letters or lines in strictly *mechanical* fashion: they are completely unaware of what they are writing or drawing, and it's as if their anaesthetized hand were being guided by another hand. Apart from those who limit themselves to such guidance, who passively witness their lines being drawn and don't understand their meaning until afterward, there are others who reproduce, as if they were tracing them, inscriptions or figures that appear to them on a given object. It would be pointless to ascribe any superiority to one or the other of these faculties, which moreover can coexist in a single individual.

In 1909, Marcel Til, a professor of accounting, communicated to Théodore Flournoy several specimens of decorative writing that he obtained via the second method, in which he received information about his son (information that proved false). Another medium, in a series of mechanical gestures, and all the while taking an active part in the ongoing conversation, rapidly covered several sheets of paper without the movements of his hand being at any time subject to his conscious control. The prodigious Elise Muller, better known as Hélène Smith, successively demonstrated automatic phenomena that were *verbo-auditory* (she noted as best she could captured fragments of fictional conversations), *vocal* (in a trance state she uttered words in an unknown tongue), *verbo-visual* (she copied exotic characters that appeared to her), and *graphic* (she wrote while completely in a trance, sometimes substituting one of her "Martian" characters for herself). We should note that in this case, which is by far the richest, only the verbo-auditory and verbo-visual automatisms left the subject a measure of critical freedom, whereas the verbo-motor automatisms completely divorced her from reality. The *Revue spirite*, which in 1858 presented the first mediumistic etching by Victorien Sardou, *Mozart's House on the Planet Jupiter*, stressed that this work, which was executed in several hours, did not originate in any preconceived idea or voluntary orientation: Sardou's hand, "guided by an occult force, moved the graver along a path that was highly irregular and counter to the most elementary principles of the art, constantly flying at phenomenal speed from one end of the plate to the other without ever leaving it, only to return to the same spot a hundred times over. Every part was thus begun and continued at the same time, without any one section being finished before another was begun. At first glance, the result was an incoherent grouping, whose end point could not be understood until the entire thing was completed." The hand of the painter Fernand Desmoulin, equally unconscious at certain moments, worked, as Jules Bois tells us, "in the dark, backward, sideways, on several parts at a time, without order, and yet imperious, clairvoyant, and knowledgeable – even if, by a precaution imposed on him by a German scientist, his face was covered by a bag, so that it could not see or direct anything. Only when the work was finished did he understand what he had done." The comte de Tromelin, an occultist whose drawings were published by Dr. Charles Guilbert in a 1913 issue of *Æsculape*, regularly began, as the author of the piece tells us, by "blackening a sheet of paper with a piece of soft black chalk cut square; he sketched out the main figure of his composition to provoke a creative idea and, after a few instants, he discerned multiple details on the black background with such clarity that he needed only trace their outlines in hard pencil. Then he used bread dough to remove the excess chalk." It is critically important to note that a good number of mediumistic drawings, including some of the most remarkable ones, were made by people "who didn't know how to draw" – Mme. Fibur, Machner, Petitjean, Lesage – and whose social occupations did not, *a priori*, leave them particularly predisposed toward exploring graphic expression. Still, it is worth recalling that Machner was a tanner, which can only remind us of Salvador Dalí's remarks on the delirious ethnographic aspect of certain skins drying in the sun; that Lesage was a miner, which creates the possibility that his eye was impressed by the structures of certain underground vaults. Just as we might admit that Postman Cheval, who remains the uncontested master of mediumistic architecture and sculpture, was haunted by the appearance of grotto floors and of the remains of petrified fountains in that area of the Drôme, where for thirty-six years he made his daily rounds on foot.

As "Scrutator" very rightly observes in the April 1910 issue of the *Occult Review,* "Anyone who remembers learning to draw a straight line or regular curve has realized that this act belongs to the order of voluntary actions. The experienced artist or draftsman knows, on the other hand, that the fact of tracing a line or curve very often falls into the domain of automatic, involuntary actions. Every action tends to become habitual, involuntary, and automatic since the first time it was done – whether it's twisting one's mustache, tossing one's hair back, satisfying one's appetite, or remembering one's name. Even a mental attitude or a way of seeing things becomes habitual and, therefore, outside of the thinker's control."

I thought it would be interesting, in one issue of a magazine* that also contained some admirable examples of art nouveau, to

* *Minotaure* 3–4.

gather a certain number of mediumistic drawings – which to my surprise, and unlike drawings by mental patients and children, had never been reproduced as a group, and could be found only occasionally in out-of-print books and generally defunct magazines. Indeed, we cannot help being struck by the affinities between these two modes of expression. What, I'm tempted to ask, is art nouveau, other than an attempt to generalize mediumistic drawing, painting, and sculpture and adapt them to the arts of furniture and building design? We find the same dissimilarity in details; the same impossibility of repetition, which is precisely what engenders the true, captivating stereotype; the same delight in endless curves, like those of young ferns, ammonite, or a curled fetus; the same meticulousness that, while exciting to behold, distracts us from enjoying the overall object, as they say that a part of time can be larger than the whole. We can therefore maintain that these two enterprises were conceived under the same sign, which could well be the sign of the *octopus* – the "octopus with silken glance," as Lautréamont said. For both, it is, in the visual sphere, the triumph of ambiguity, even in the lines themselves; and in the interpretative sphere, the triumph of the complex, even to the point of insignificance. These two modes of expression, which theoretically respond to such divergent needs for externalization, even share (and repeat ad nauseam) the use of subjects that are or are not incidental to the vegetable kingdom, as well as a tendency to evoke, superficially but unmistakably, certain productions of ancient Asian or Native American art.

If the various samples of mediumistic automatic writing occasionally offered to our curious eyes are hardly as interesting as the drawings that derive from the same source, it must be said that the fault lies in annoying spiritualistic texts that, to a large degree, have contaminated these writings from the start. We know in fact that the entire effort of such literature has been toward justifying and proclaiming the exogenous dictating principle, in other words (since clarity forces us to use such nauseating terminology) the existence of "spirits." Not that this unreasonable belief has bypassed the visual mediums: Victorien Sardou believed he was drawing and engraving under the direction of Bernard Palissy; Hélène Smith, even in daily life, acted only on the advice of "Leopold"; Léon Petitjean executed his portraits of "spirits dressed in their fluid costumes" under the influence of his mother's ghost. But without a doubt, it is especially in the written domain that this deplorable joke has followed its degrading course, which was furthered with the ill-conceived support of the Hugo family and their story of the "séance tables of Guernsey." I consider it best to say nothing about these productions (whose hypothetical nature only makes them sketchier), which are predetermined by the hope of obtaining some word from the "beyond," of gaining the help of some long-dead great man whose voice can be recognized by its tone of scholarly recitation; productions that moreover have nothing in common save their bombast and the way they flatter such appalling naiveté.

Mlle. X, schoolmistress and mediumistic author, in an 1895 brochure on "the perplexities of a conscientious medium" – although she doesn't escape the rule mentioned above (she received her communications from "thinkers" such as Calvin, Amiel, Hugo, Quinet, etc., but especially from her dead brother) – proved especially adept at analyzing what she felt when she lent herself to automatic dictation, and she left behind precious information on the evolution of her faculties. "My mediumism," she said, "has altered considerably over these eight years of practice. At first, I was absolutely unaware of what my hand was going to write; it moved as if guided by another hand. Little by little, this impulse diminished, and I acquired the ability to perceive the thought I had to write down. It is now very difficult for me to write when I do not perceive the dictated thought and I hardly feel any mechanical impulse, except when I begin, and also when my hand traces the final line to warn me that the dictation is finished, as if saying, 'I have spoken.' I greatly miss my initial automatism, but the transformation happened without me and in spite of me, and was accompanied by other losses that I also deplore." These remarks, which describe the gradual loss of the mediumistic faculty through a progressive transformation from verbo-motor automatism to verbo-auditory automatism, are corroborated by the answers Marcel Til and Professor Cuendet gave Théodore Flournoy, and that the latter published in *Esprits et Médiums*. The striking thing is that all three of them mention the same regret, express the same nostalgia.

The term "automatic writing," as it is used in Surrealism, is (as we have seen) subject to debate. If I can be held partly responsible for that impropriety, it's because "automatic" writing (or "mechanical writing," as Flournoy puts it; or rather "unconscious writing," as René Sudre prefers) has always seemed to me the limit toward which the Surrealist poet must strive, while not losing sight of the fact that, contrary to what spiritualism aims to do – dissociate the psychological personality from the medium – Surrealism proposes nothing less than to unify that personality. It is obvious that, for us, the question of the exteriority of (let's say, for simplicity's sake) one's "voice" could not even be posed. Furthermore, from the outset it seemed needlessly difficult and, considering the extrapsychological aspects of the goal we were pursuing, almost superfluous for us to get bogged down in a division of so-called inspired writing – which we set in opposition to calculated literature – into "mechanical," "semi-mechanical," and "intuitive" writing: these three qualifiers account for no more than differences of degree. Once again, our only choice was to head as far as possible down a trail that had been blazed by Lautréamont and Rimbaud (as to the latter, I need only cite as manifest proof the first line of his poem "Promontory"), and that had become particularly attractive thanks to certain procedures of psychoanalytic investigation. In the twentieth century, right after the war, this trail necessarily wound past the small group of poets that we formed; and when we began following it, we suddenly became aware of murmurs stretching behind and before us as far as the eye could see. We know that the attempt to capture written automatic messages was soon joined by another process that tried to capture this message in its spoken form. But on this point, our experiments fully justified Myers's claim that automatic *speech* does not in itself constitute a more developed form of the motor message than automatic *writing*, and that moreover it is to be feared because of the profound changes in memory and personality it can bring about.

Surrealism's distinctive feature is to have proclaimed the total equality of all normal human beings before the subliminal message, to have constantly maintained that this message constitutes a common patrimony, of which everyone is entitled to a share, and which must very soon, and at all costs, stop being seen as the prerogative of the chosen few. I say that every man and every woman deserves to be convinced of their ability to tap into this language at will, which has nothing supernatural about it and which, for each and every one of us, is *the* vehicle of revelation. In order to do this, it is crucial that they revise their narrow and erroneous conception of such specific vocations, whether artistic or mediumistic. If one looked closely, one would in fact discover that every vocation has originated in a fortuitous accident, whose effect has been to undermine certain resistances in the individual. For whoever is concerned with something other than his prosaic, immediate interest, the essential thing is that these resistances can be undermined. As Professor Lipps observes in his study of the automatic dances performed by the medium Magdeleine around 1908, "Hypnosis is never more than the negative reason for the talents manifested under its influence; their true source lies in pre-existing tendencies, faculties, or dispositions, which were diverted from their natural expression by contrary factors. The role of hypnosis is simply to free these talents by paralyzing those factors." Automatic writing – which is easy and attractive, and which we hoped to put within *everyone's* reach by eliminating the unnerving and cumbersome apparatus of hypnosis – seems, regardless of such obstacles, to be what Schrenck-Notzing wanted to see it as, namely, "a sure means of favoring the outpouring of psychic faculties, and particularly artistic talents, by focusing one's consciousness on the task at hand and by freeing the individual from the inhibitory factors that restrain and trouble him, sometimes utterly blocking the exercise of his latent gifts."

This standpoint of artistic talent, and the incredible vanity that goes along with it, is naturally a large part of the internal and external causes of distrust that, in Surrealism, have prevented automatic writing from fulfilling all its promises. Although the original aim was simply to seize involuntary verbal representations in their continuity and fix them in writing, while avoiding any qualitative judgments, critical comparisons could not avoid showing that the internal language of different writers displayed unequal levels of richness and elegance – which was fertile terrain for despicable poetic rivalries. In most cases, furthermore, an inevitable, subsequent delight in the very terms of the texts obtained, and specifically in the images and symbolic figures with which they abounded, also helped undermine the indifference and distraction that these authors needed to maintain toward their texts (at least while producing them). This attitude, instinctive on the part of those who are practiced in judging poetic value, had the unfortunate result of giving the recording subject an immediate hold over each part of the recorded message. And so ended the cycle of what Dr. Georges Petit, in an utterly remarkable work, called "apperceptive self-representations," *on which,* by definition, *we still propose to act by relating them, with no possible ambiguity, to the Ego.* For us, the result was a barely intermittent succession of visual images that occurred during the very act of listening, interrupting the murmur, and that, to the latter's great detriment, we could not always resist capturing. Let me explain. Not only do I think that there is almost always complexity in imaginary sounds – the unity and speed of the dictation remain active concerns – but it also seems certain that visual or tactile images (primitive, not preceded or accompanied by words, like the representation of whiteness or elasticity without any prior, concomitant, or subsequent intervention of words that express them or derive from them) freely operate in the immeasurable region that stretches between consciousness and unconsciousness. Now, if automatic dictation can be obtained with a certain continuity, the process by which these images develop and join together is very difficult to grasp. As far as we can tell, their nature is eruptive. So it was that on the very evening (September 27) that I noted the two sentences at the beginning of this article, just when I had given up in my subsequent attempts to provoke a verbal equivalent, I suddenly saw myself (my hand?) rolling the edges – as one does to prepare a paper filter – or reducing the sides of a kind of scallop shell. Without a doubt, I took this as another form of automatism. Was it obtained in compensation for the verbal one that I was trying too hard to hear? I don't know. Nonetheless (and this is the main thing), I consider verbal inspirations infinitely richer in visual meaning, infinitely more resistant to the eye, than visual images properly speaking. Whence my constant protest against the poet's so-called "visionary" power. No, Lautréamont and Rimbaud did not *see*, did not experience *a priori* what they described; which is tantamount to saying that they didn't describe it at all, but rather that they limited themselves in the dark corridors of their being to listening – indistinctly and, while they wrote, without understanding them any more than we do when we first read them – to certain accomplished and accomplishable works. "Illumination" comes *afterward*.

In poetry, verbo-auditory automatism has always seemed to me to create the most thrilling visual images for the reader. Verbo-visual automatism has never seemed to me to create visual images that are in any way comparable. Suffice it to say that today, as ten years ago, I am entirely devoted to, and continue to believe blindly in (blindly… with a blindness that simultaneously covers all visual things), the triumph *of the auditory* over the unverifiable visual.

Now that I've made my point, it goes without saying that the floor should be turned over to the painters, contradiction or not.

To my great regret, I can only outline here the history of the crisis that the Surrealist attitude, vis-à-vis the degree of reality granted the *object*, cannot help imposing under such conditions on purely speculative thought. Poets and artists, theologians, psychologists, the mentally ill, and psychiatrists, moreover, have always sought a valid demarcation line between imaginary objects and real ones, all the while recognizing that the latter can easily disappear from the field of awareness and the former appear there; that subjectively their properties have proven to be interchangeable. Automatic writing, when practiced fervently, leads directly to visual hallucinations: I had the experience myself, and a quick glance at "Alchemy of the Verb" will show that Rimbaud had it long before me. But I have a hard time understanding why there was such "terror" in his renunciation. I know of few psychological texts as disillusioned and, by the same token, as pathetic as the sentence that ends the two volumes of Pierre Quercy's recent, fundamental work, *L'Hallucination,* which with one very pessimistic observation temporarily puts an end to interminable disputes between mystics and nonmystics, patients and doctors, the (fanatical) partisans of "objectless perception" and those of "the image baptized perception": "One can affirm the presence or perception of an object when it is present and perceived, when it is absent and perceived, and when it is neither present nor perceived." The degree of spontaneity that a given individual is capable of alone determines for him whether a pan on the scale will fall or rise... The "derangement" of the senses, of all the senses, remains to be achieved; or – and this comes down to the same thing – the education (in reality, the diseducation) of all the senses remains to be done.

In this regard, we cannot fail to pay special attention to the recent efforts of the Marburg school, even though they continue to arouse some very bitter disputes. According to the masters of this school (Kiesov, Jaensch), remarkable aptitudes can be cultivated in children, which consist in being able to change a given object into *anything at all* simply by staring at it. The researchers claim that removing an object which the child has studied for fifteen seconds induces the formation, not of a vague, quickly fading afterimage whose color is complementary to the studied object, but of a so-called *eidetic* (aesthetic) image, which is sharply defined, possesses a great wealth of detail, and is the same color as the object itself. This image is infinitely variable, and shows some characteristic infidelities vis-à-vis the model: "If we show the child the silhouette of a horse, head erect and a rider on his back, as an eidetic image the horse could very well be grazing and the horseman could be in his saddle facing the animal's tail. If we show the subject an F, he might see an ꟻ, an Ⅎ, or even an ꓒ, and the horse he saw earlier might reappear with its four hooves in the air." (We can't help thinking of Chagall's early canvases.) All of these ongoing experiments tend to demonstrate that perception and representation – which to ordinary adults seem so radically opposed – should be seen as products resulting from the dissociation of a *single, original faculty*, which the eidetic image translates, and of which we find traces in primitive peoples and children. Anyone wishing to define the true human condition aspires more or less vaguely to recover this state of grace. I say that only automatism can lead to it. One can systematically, safe from any delirium, work toward depriving the distinction between the subjective and the objective of its necessity and its value. "There is," said Myers, so strange a "form of inward hearing... There exist complex and powerful groupings of concepts formed outside of (some say beyond) articulated language and reasoned thought. There is a path, an ascension across ideal spaces that some see as the only true ascension; there is an architecture that some consider the one true dwelling..."

Simply by virtue of the fact that she saw her wooden cross transform into a crucifix made of precious stones, and that she held this vision to be at once *imaginative and sensorial*, Saint Teresa of Ávila can be said to command the line along which mediums and poets take their place. Unfortunately, she's still only a saint.

December 1933

Sources and Acknowledgments

INTRODUCTION TO THE DISCOURSE ON THE PAUCITY OF REALITY
First published as "Introduction au discours sur le peu de réalité" in *Commerce* 3 (winter 1924) and as a separate pamphlet by Editions Gallimard in 1927. The actual "Discourse" promised by the title was never written.

BURIAL DENIED
First published as "Défense d'inhumer" as part of the collective broadside *Un Cadavre* [A corpse], issued on October 18, 1924. Intended to coincide with Anatole France's death nearly a week before, the pamphlet was delayed by a nervous printer.

IN SELF-DEFENSE
First published as *Légitime défense* in a limited-edition pamphlet on September 30, 1926. Reprinted in *La Révolution surréaliste* 8 (1 December 1926).

Excerpt from Keyserling translated by J. Holroyd Reece, in Count Hermann Keyserling, *The Travel Diary of a Philosopher,* vol. I (New York: Harcourt, Brace & Company, 1925), p. 338.

PAUL ELUARD'S CAPITAL OF PAIN
First published as a publisher's loose-leaf blurb to be inserted in copies of Paul Eluard's *Capitale de la douleur* (Paris: Gallimard, 1926).

THE X..., Y... EXHIBIT
First published as the preface to the exhibition catalogue *Exposition Delbrouck et M. Defize* (Paris, April 1929). Perhaps to make his comments seem more general, Breton eliminated the two artists' names when including the piece in the present volume.

NOTICE TO THE READER OF THE HUNDRED HEADLESS WOMAN
First published as the preface to Max Ernst's *La Femme 100 Têtes* (Paris: Editions du Carrefour, 1929).

THE FIRST DALÍ EXHIBIT
First published as an untitled text in the exhibition catalogue *Dalí* (Paris, November–December 1929).

LYUBOVNAYA LODKA RAZBILAS O BYT
First published in *Le Surréalisme au service de la Révolution* 1 [henceforth *SASDLR*] (July 1930).

ON THE RELATIONS BETWEEN INTELLECTUAL LABOR AND CAPITAL
First published as "Rapports du travail intellectuel et du capital" in *SASDLR* 2 (October 1930).

Excerpts from *Capital* translated by Samuel Moore and Edward Aveling, in Karl Marx, *Capital: A Critique of Political Economy* (New York: Modern Library, 1906), pp. 47–48.

PSYCHIATRY STANDING BEFORE SURREALISM
First published as "La Médecine mentale devant le surréalisme" in *SASDLR* 2 (October 1930).

Excerpt from *Nadja* translated by Richard Howard, in André Breton, *Nadja* (New York: Grove Press, 1960). The remarks by Janet and Clérambault are translated by Richard Seaver and Helen R. Lane, in André Breton, *Manifestoes of Surrealism* (Ann Arbor: University of Michigan Press, 1969).

LETTER TO ANDRÉ ROLLAND DE RENÉVILLE
First published in the "Correspondence" pages of *La Nouvelle Revue française* (July 1932).

ON THE PROLETARIAN LITERATURE CONTEST SPONSORED BY L'HUMANITÉ
First published as "A propos du concours de littérature prolétarienne organisé par *L'Humanité*" in *SASDLR* 5 (May 1933), from a lecture given by Breton on February 23, 1933, at a meeting of the Association des Ecrivains et Artistes Révolutionnaires, of which he was a board member. The published version represents less than half the original lecture, the excised portions mainly concerning specifics about the contest and the submissions received.

Excerpt from *What Is to Be Done?* translated by George Fineberg and George Hanna, in V. I. Lenin, *What Is to Be Done? Burning Questions of Our Movement* (New York: International Publishers, 1969), pp. 40–41.

Excerpt from *The Tasks of the Youth Leagues* [trans. unknown], in Robert C. Tucker, ed., *The Lenin Anthology* (New York: W. W. Norton, 1975), p. 664.

Excerpt from Engels's letter to Eduard Bernstein translated by Lee Baxandall and Stefan Morawski, in Karl Marx and Frederick Engels, *On Literature and Art: A Selection of Writings* (St. Louis and Milwaukee: Telos Press, 1973), p. 123 (where the letter is dated 1881).

INTRODUCTION TO ACHIM VON ARNIM'S STRANGE TALES
First published as the introduction to *Contes bizarres* (Paris: Editions des Cahiers Libres, 1933). A long excerpt from it also appeared in *SASDLR* 6 (May 1933).

PICASSO IN HIS ELEMENT
First published as "Picasso dans son élément" in *Minotaure* 1 (June 1933).

THE FACES OF WOMEN
First published as "Les Visages de la Femme" in the volume *Man Ray: Photographs 1920–1934 Paris* (Hartford, Conn.: James Thrall Soby; Paris: Editions des Cahiers d'Art, 1934).

THE AUTOMATIC MESSAGE
First published as "Le Message automatique" in *Minotaure* 3–4 (December 1933).

André Breton
Mad Love
translated by Mary Ann Caws

Blaise Cendrars
Modernities and Other Writings
edited by Monique Chefdor
translated by Esther Allen and Monique Chefdor

The Cubist Poets in Paris: An Anthology
edited by L. C. Breunig

René Daumal
You've Always Been Wrong
translated by Thomas Vosteen

Max Jacob
Hesitant Fire: Selected Prose of Max Jacob
translated and edited by Moishe Black and Maria Green

Jean Paulhan
Progress in Love on the Slow Side
translated by Christine Moneera Laennec and Michael Syrotinski

Benjamin Péret
Death to the Pigs, and Other Writings
translated by Rachel Stella and others

Boris Vian
Blues for a Black Cat and Other Stories
edited and translated by Julia Older

www.ingramcontent.com/pod-product-compliance
Ingram Content Group UK Ltd.
Pitfield, Milton Keynes, MK11 3LW, UK
UKHW032058180225
455276UK00001B/4

9 780803 220843